The Complete
FAMILY
COOKBOOK

The Complete

Alex Barker

The Complete

FAMILY
COOKBOOK

Alex Barker

OVER 130 EASY-TO-PREPARE RECIPES

SMITHMARK

This edition published in 1994
by SMITHMARK Publishers Inc.
16 East 32nd Street
New York
NY 10016
USA

SMITHMARK books are available for bulk purchase for sales and
promotion and premium use. For details write or call the manager of
special sales,
SMITHMARK Publishers Inc.
16 East 32nd Street
New York
NY 100016
(212) 532-6600

Editorial Director: Joanna Lorenz
Series Editor: Linda Fraser
Designers: Tony Paine and Roy Prescott
Photographer: Steve Baxter
Food for Photography: Carole Handslip
Props Stylist: Blake Minton

Printed and bound in Singapore

CONTENTS

SOUPS

Soups can be richly warming and substantial, perfect for the starving hordes on a cold winter's night – tempt young members of the family with Chicken Broth with Cheese Toasts, or Creamy Carrot Soup. Look again at their potential as meals in themselves rather than just gap fillers. Soups can be so filling and tasty that they make a perfect light lunch – try a hearty bowl of Chunky Pasta Soup served with pesto croûtons, or a slice or two of crusty bread. Soups make for very easy, relaxed entertaining too, ready to serve when you want with little or no last minute fussing or cooking – ideal are the Mussel Bisque, Watercress and Orange Soup, and Mushroom and Herb Soup.

CHUNKY PASTA SOUP

Serve this hearty main-meal soup with tasty, pesto-topped French bread croûtons.

INGREDIENTS

Serves 4

⅔ cup dry beans (a mixture of red kidney and haricot beans), soaked in cold water overnight
1 tbsp oil
1 onion, chopped
2 celery stalks, thinly sliced
2–3 garlic cloves, crushed
2 leeks, thinly sliced
1 vegetable bouillon cube
14oz can or jar of pimientos
3–4 tbsp tomato paste
4oz pasta shapes
4 pieces French bread
1 tbsp pesto sauce
1 cup baby corn, halved
2oz each broccoli and cauliflower florets
few drops of Tabasco sauce, to taste
salt and black pepper

1 Drain the beans and place in a large pan with 5 cups water. Bring to a boil and simmer for about 1 hour, or until nearly tender.

2 When the beans are almost ready, heat the oil in a large pan and fry the vegetables for 2 minutes. Add the bouillon cube and the beans with about 2 cups of their liquid. Cover and simmer for 10 minutes.

3 Meanwhile, purée the pimientos with a little of their liquid and add to the pan. Stir in the tomato paste and pasta and cook for 15 minutes. Preheat the oven to 400°F.

4 Meanwhile, make the pesto croûtons; spread the French bread with the pesto sauce and bake for 10 minutes, or until crispy.

5 When the pasta is just cooked, add the corn, broccoli and cauliflower florets, Tabasco sauce and seasoning to taste. Heat through for 2–3 minutes and serve at once with the pesto croûtons.

MUSSEL BISQUE

Served hot, this makes a delicious and very filling soup, perfect for a light, lunch-time meal. It is also excellent cold.

INGREDIENTS

Serves 6
1½ lb fresh mussels in their shells
⅔ cup dry white wine or cider
2 tbsp butter
1 small red onion, chopped
1 small leek, thinly sliced
1 carrot, finely diced
2 tomatoes, skinned, seeded and
   chopped
2 garlic cloves, crushed
1 tbsp chopped fresh parsley
1tbsp chopped fresh basil
1 celery stalk, finely sliced
½ red pepper, seeded and chopped
1 cup whipping cream
salt and black pepper

1 Scrub the mussels and pull off the beards. Discard any broken ones, or any that don't close when tapped. Place them in a large pan with half the wine and ⅔ cup water.

2 Cover and cook the mussels over a high heat until they open up. (Discard any which don't open.) Transfer the mussels with a draining spoon to another dish and leave until cool enough to handle. Remove the mussels from their shells; leaving a few in their shells, to garnish if you like.

3 Strain the stock through a piece of cheesecloth or a fine cloth to get rid of any grit. Heat the butter in the same large pan and cook the onion, leek, carrot, tomatoes and garlic over a high heat for 2–3 minutes.

4 Reduce the heat and cook for a further 2–3 minutes, then add the cooking liquid, 1¼ cups water and the herbs and simmer for a further 10 minutes. Add the mussels, celery, peppers, cream, and seasoning to taste. Serve hot.

Chicken Broth with Cheese Toasts

Serves 4

1 roasted chicken carcass
1 onion, quartered
2 celery stalks, finely chopped
1 garlic clove, crushed
few sprigs parsley
2 bay leaves
8oz can chopped tomatoes
14oz can chick-peas
2–3 tbsp leftover vegetables, chopped,
   or 1 large carrot, finely chopped
1 tbsp chopped fresh parsley
2 slices toast
¼ cup grated cheese
salt and black pepper

1 Pick off any little bits of meat from the carcass, especially from the underside where there is often some very tasty dark meat. Put aside.

2 Place the carcass, broken in half, in a large pan with the onion, half the celery, the garlic, herbs and sufficient water to cover. Cover the pan, bring to a boil and simmer for about 30 minutes, or until you are left with about 1¼ cups of liquid.

3 Strain the stock and return to the pan. Add the chicken meat, the remaining celery, the tomatoes, chickpeas (and their liquid), vegetables and parsley. Season to taste and simmer for another 7–10 minutes.

4 Meanwhile, sprinkle the toast with the cheese and grill until bubbling. Cut the toast into fingers or quarters and serve with, or floating on top of, the finished soup.

Bread and Cheese Soup

Serves 4

4oz strong-flavored or blue cheese, or
   6oz mild cheese
2¼ cups semi-skimmed milk
few pinches ground mace
4–6 slices stale bread
2 tbsp olive oil
1 large garlic clove, crushed
salt and black pepper
1 tbsp snipped chives, to garnish

1 Remove any rinds from the cheese and grate into a heavy-based, preferably non-stick pan. Add the milk and heat through very slowly, stirring frequently to make sure it does not stick and burn.

2 When all the cheese has melted, add the mace, seasoning, and one piece of crustless bread. Cook over a very gentle heat until the bread has softened and slightly thickened the soup.

3 Mix the oil with the garlic and brush over the remaining bread. Toast until crisp, then cut into triangles or fingers. Sprinkle the soup with chives and serve with the toast.

> **Cook's Tip**
> Don't mix blue cheeses with other kinds of cheese in this soup.

CARROT AND CORIANDER SOUP

Carrot soup is best made with young carrots when they are at their sweetest and tastiest. With older carrots you will have to use more to get the full flavor. This soup freezes well.

INGREDIENTS

Serves 5–6
1 onion, chopped
1 tbsp sunflower oil
1½ lb carrots, chopped
3¼ cups chicken stock
few sprigs cilantro, or 1 tsp dried
1 tsp lemon rind
2 tbsp lemon juice
salt and black pepper
chopped fresh parsley or coriander, to garnish

1 Soften the onion in the oil in a large pan. Add the chopped carrots, the stock, cilantro, lemon rind and juice and seasoning to taste.

2 Bring to the boil, cover and simmer for 15–20 minutes, occasionally checking that there is sufficient liquid. When the carrots are really tender, blend or process and return to the pan, then check the seasoning.

3 Heat through again and sprinkle with chopped parsley or cilantro before serving.

SHRIMP AND CORN CHOWDER

This soup is perfect for informal entertaining as it is quite special but not too extravagant.

INGREDIENTS

Serves 4
1 tbsp butter
1 onion, chopped
11oz can corn
2 tbsp lemon juice
1¼ cups fish or vegetable stock
1 cup cooked, peeled shrimp
1¼ cups milk
1–2 tbsp cream or yogurt
salt and black pepper
4 large shrimp in their shells and a few sprigs parsley or dill, to garnish

1 Heat the butter in a pan and cook the onions until translucent. Add half the corn and all its liquid, the lemon juice, stock and half the shrimp.

2 Cover and simmer the soup for about 15 minutes, then blend or process the soup until quite smooth.

3 Return the soup to the pan and add the milk, the rest of the shrimp, chopped, and the corn, the cream or yogurt and seasoning to taste. Cook gently for 5 minutes, or until reduced sufficiently.

4 Serve each portion garnished with a whole shrimp and a herb sprig.

Watercress and Orange Soup

This is a very healthy and refreshing soup, which is just as good served hot or chilled.

Ingredients

Serves 4

1 large onion, chopped
1 tbsp olive oil
2 bunches or bags of watercress
grated rind and juice of 1 large orange
1 vegetable bouillon cube
⅔ cup light cream
2 tsp cornstarch
salt and black pepper
a little thick cream or yogurt, to garnish
4 orange wedges, to serve

1 Soften the onion in the oil in a large pan. Trim any big stems off the watercress, then add to the pan of onion without chopping. Cover the pan and cook the watercress for about 5 minutes until softened.

2 Add the orange rind and juice, and the bouillon cube dissolved in 2½ cups water. Bring to a boil, cover and simmer for 10–15 minutes.

3 Blend or process the soup thoroughly, and sieve if you like. Add the cream blended with the cornstarch, and seasoning to taste.

4 Bring the soup gently back to a boil, stirring until just slightly thickened. Check the seasoning and serve the soup with a swirl of cream or yogurt, and a wedge of orange to squeeze in at the last moment.

> COOK'S TIP
> Wash the watercress only if really necessary, it is often very clean.

MUSHROOM AND HERB SOUP

Although you can make mushroom soup with a nice smooth texture, it is more time consuming and you waste a lot of mushrooms – so enjoy the slightly nutty consistency instead!

INGREDIENTS

Serves 4
2oz hickory smoked bacon
1 white onion, chopped
1 tbsp sunflower oil
*12oz flat cap field mushrooms or a
 mixture of wild and brown
 mushrooms*
2½ cups good meat stock
2 tbsp sweet sherry
*2 tbsp chopped, mixed fresh herbs,
 such as sage, rosemary, thyme or
 marjoram, or 2 tsp dried*
salt and black pepper
*4 tbsp thick Greek-style yogurt or
 crème fraîche and a few sprigs of
 marjoram or sage, to garnish*

1 Coarsely chop the bacon and place in a large saucepan. Cook gently until all the fat comes out of the bacon.

2 Add the onion and soften, adding oil if necessary. Wipe the mushrooms clean, coarsely chop and add to the pan. Cover and sweat until they have completely softened and their liquid has run out.

3 Add the stock, sherry, herbs and seasoning, cover and simmer for 10–12 minutes. Blend or process the soup until smooth, but don't worry if you still have a slightly textured result.

4 Check the seasoning and heat through. Serve with a dollop of yogurt or crème fraîche and a herb sprig in each bowl.

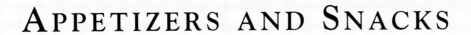

APPETIZERS AND SNACKS

Nowadays, appetizers are rarely served at mealtimes, except perhaps at weekends, or during the holidays, and when entertaining. However, snacks such as dips, nice nibbles, and any-time-of-the-day foods are always in demand. This is a general selection suitable for all sorts of occasions. The appetizers include fancy weekend classics such as Chicken, Bacon and Walnut Terrine, and Tandoori Shrimp-filled Avocados, while the snacks range from lunch box favorites of Tuna Croissants, and Tomato and Garlic Stuffed Muffins to a rich and delicious version of cheese on toast – the Three-Cheese Croûtes; and a popular kids' filler-upper – Mushroom Popovers.

LEEK AND BROCCOLI TARTLETS

INGREDIENTS

Serves 4

1½ cups flour, sifted
½ cup butter
1oz finely grated pecorino cheese or
   young, mild Parmesan
2 small leeks, sliced
3oz tiny broccoli florets
⅔ cup milk
2 eggs
2 tbsp heavy cream
few pinches ground mace
salt and black pepper
2 tbsp slivered almonds, toasted, to
   garnish

1 Blend the flour, butter and cheese together in a food processor to give a fine crumb consistency. Add salt to taste. Stir in 4–6 tbsp cold water and bring the pastry together in a ball. Chill for 15 minutes.

2 Preheat the oven to 375°F. Roll out the pastry on a floured surface and use to line four 4in tartlet pans. Line the pastry shells with greaseproof paper and fill with baking beans. Bake them for 15 minutes, then remove the paper and beans and cook for a further 5 minutes to dry out the bases.

3 To make the filling, place the vegetables in a pan and cook them in the milk for 2–3 minutes. Strain the milk into a small bowl and whisk in the eggs, mace, seasoning and cream.

4 Arrange the vegetables in the pastry cases and pour over the egg mixture. Bake for 20 minutes, or until the filling is just firm. Sprinkle with almonds before serving.

> **COOK'S TIP**
> Cook and freeze the tartlet cases, ready for easy weekend meals. They only need 15 minutes defrosting. Use other colorful, crunchy vegetables in season.

RICE AND CHEESE CROQUETTES

Although you can use leftover cooked rice here, freshly cooked rice is easier to work with. The garlicky mayonnaise aïoli makes a good dip for crudités too.

INGREDIENTS

Makes about 16
½ cup long grain rice, cooked
2 eggs, lightly beaten
3oz mozzarella or Bel Paese cheese, grated
½ cup fine dry breadcrumbs
salt and black pepper
oil, for frying

For the aïoli
1 egg yolk
few drops of lemon juice or vinegar
1 large garlic clove, crushed
1 cup good salad oil

1 Drain the cooked rice thoroughly and allow to cool slightly, then mix in the eggs, cheese and seasoning.

2 Mold the rice mixture with your hands into 16 equal sized balls and coat in breadcrumbs, pressing on the crumbs well. Chill for 20 minutes.

3 Meanwhile, make the aïoli; beat together the egg yolk, lemon juice, garlic and seasoning. Gradually whisk in sufficient oil to make a thick, glossy mayonnaise. Chill until ready to serve.

4 Heat the oil in a frying pan until almost hazy, then cook the rice balls, in two batches, for 4–5 minutes each, or until crisp and golden all over.

5 Drain the rice balls on kitchen paper as soon as they are cooked and keep warm until required (or reheat in a hot oven) before serving with the garlic dip.

COOK'S TIP
These are very good if you give them a surprise center – try chunks of ham, olives or nuts.

HERB OMELETTE WITH TOMATO SALAD

This is ideal as a snack or a light lunch – use flavorful, fresh plum tomatoes in season.

INGREDIENTS

Serves 4

4 eggs, beaten
2 tbsp chopped, mixed fresh herbs,
   such as chives, marjoram, thyme or
   parsley, or 2 tsp dried
1 tbsp butter
3–4 tbsp olive oil
1 tbsp fresh orange juice
1 tsp red wine vinegar
1 tsp grainy mustard
2 large tomatoes, thinly sliced
salt and black pepper
fresh herb sprigs, to garnish

1 Beat the eggs, herbs and seasoning together. Heat the butter and a little of the oil in an omelette pan.

2 When the fats are just sizzling, pour in the egg mixture and leave to set, stirring very occasionally with a fork. This omelette needs to be almost cooked through (about 5 minutes).

3 Meanwhile, heat the rest of the oil in a small pan with the orange juice, vinegar and mustard, and add salt and pepper to taste.

4 Roll up the cooked omelette and neatly cut into ½ in wide strips. Keep them rolled up and transfer immediately to the hot plates.

5 Arrange the sliced tomatoes on the plates with the omelette rolls and pour on the warm dressing. Garnish with herb sprigs and serve at once.

THREE-CHEESE CROÛTES

INGREDIENTS

Serves 2–4

4 thick slices of slightly stale bread
little butter, or mustard
3oz Brie
3 tbsp ricotta
2oz grated Parmesan or mature
   Cheddar
1 small garlic clove, crushed
salt and black pepper
black olives, to garnish

COOK'S TIP
If you have Brie which will not ripen fully, this is an excellent way of using it up. You'll need a knife and fork to eat this snack!

1 Preheat the oven to 400°F. Place the bread slices on a baking sheet, close together, and spread with either a little butter or mustard.

2 Cut the Brie into thin slices or pieces and arrange the slices or pieces evenly on the bread.

3 Mix together the ricotta, Parmesan or Cheddar, garlic, and seasoning to taste. Spread over the Brie and the bread to the corners.

4 Bake for 10–15 minutes, or until golden and bubbling. Serve immediately, garnished with black olives.

CHICKEN, BACON AND WALNUT TERRINE

Serves 8–10

2 boneless chicken breast portions
1 large garlic clove, crushed
½ slice bread
1 egg
12oz smoked pork chops, minced or
* finely chopped*
8oz chicken or turkey livers,
* finely chopped*
¼ cup chopped walnuts, toasted
2 tbsp sweet sherry or Madeira
½ tsp ground allspice
½ tsp cayenne pepper
pinch each ground nutmeg and
* cloves*
8 long rashers bacon, rinded and
* stretched*
salt and black pepper
chicory leaves and chives, to garnish

1 Cut the chicken breasts into thin strips and season lightly. Mash the garlic, bread and egg together. Work in the chopped pork (using your hands is really the best way) and then the finely chopped livers. Stir in the chopped walnuts, sherry or Madeira, spices and seasoning to taste.

2 Preheat the oven to 400°F. Line a 1½ lb loaf pan with the bacon rashers and pack in half the meat mixture. Lay the chicken strips on the top and spread the rest of the mixture over. Cover the loaf pan with lightly greased foil, seal well and press down firmly.

3 Place the terrine in a roasting pan half full of hot water and bake for 1–1½ hours, or until firm to the touch. Remove from the oven and place weights on the top and leave to cool completely. Drain off any excess fat or liquid while the terrine is warm.

4 When really cold, turn out the terrine, cut into thick slices and serve at once, garnished with a few chicory leaves and chives.

> **COOK'S TIP**
> If you wish to seal the terrine for longer storage, pour melted shortening over, while it is in its pan. Leave to set and form a complete seal.

MONDAY SAVORY OMELETTE

Here is a very tasty way to use up leftover meat, vegetables, rice, or pasta from the weekend.

INGREDIENTS

Serves 4–6

2 tbsp olive oil
1 large onion, chopped
2 large garlic cloves, crushed
4oz bacon, rinds removed, and chopped
½ cup cold cooked meat, chopped
¾ cup leftover cooked vegetables (preferably ones which are not too soft)
½ cup leftover cooked rice or pasta
4 eggs
2 tbsp chopped, mixed fresh herbs, such as parsley, chives, marjoram or tarragon, or 2 tsp dried
1 tsp Worcestershire sauce, or more to taste
1 tbsp grated mature Cheddar cheese
salt and black pepper

1 Heat the oil in a large flameproof frying pan and sauté the onion, garlic and bacon until all the fat has run out of the bacon.

2 Add the chopped meat, vegetables and rice. Beat the eggs, herbs and Worcestershire sauce together with seasoning. Pour over the rice or pasta and vegetables, stir slightly, then leave the omelette mixture undisturbed to cook gently for about 5 minutes.

3 When beginning to set, sprinkle with cheese and place under the grill until just firm and golden.

COOK'S TIP
This is surprisingly good cold, so is perfect for taking on picnics, or using for lunch boxes.

TANDOORI SHRIMP–FILLED AVOCADOS

Make this shrimp mixture quite spicy so it contrasts well with the cool, creamy avocados.

INGREDIENTS

Serves 4

4 tbsp good mayonnaise
4 tbsp Greek-style yogurt
2 tsp lemon juice
1 tsp tandoori paste or tandoori spice mix
6oz shelled shrimp
2 large or 4 small firm, ripe avocados
salt and black pepper
sprigs of fresh herbs, to garnish

1 Mix together the mayonnaise, yogurt, 1 tsp lemon juice, tandoori paste or spice mix, and add seasoning to taste. Stir in the shrimp and set aside until ready to serve.

2 Halve the avocados, remove the stones and brush the flesh with a little lemon juice.

3 Spoon the shrimp mixture into the avocado halves and garnish with herbs. Serve with crisp triangles of Melba toast, or pita bread.

COOK'S TIP
If you use frozen shrimp, defrost them well and drain thoroughly before mixing them with the spicy mayonnaise.

BAKED EGGPLANT SLICES

INGREDIENTS

Serves 4

3–4 tbsp olive oil
1 large eggplant
1 large or 2 medium tomatoes, thickly sliced
few basil leaves, shredded
4oz mozzarella cheese, sliced
salt and black pepper

1 Preheat the oven to 375°F. Brush a baking sheet with a very little oil. Trim the eggplant and cut lengthways into slices about ¼in thick. Arrange the eggplant slices on the greased sheet.

2 Brush the eggplant slices liberally with oil and sprinkle with seasoning. Arrange tomato slices on top of each eggplant slice and then add half of the shredded basil.

3 Top with the cheese and another light brushing of oil. Bake for 15 minutes, or until the eggplant is tender and the cheese is bubbling and golden.

COOK'S TIP
These eggplant slices are substantial enough to be served as a light lunch, or as part of a vegetarian meal. Use chopped fresh parsley in place of the basil leaves, if you prefer.

SMOKED MACKEREL AND APPLE DIP

Serve this quick fish dip with tasty, curried dippers.

INGREDIENTS

Serves 6–8
12oz smoked mackerel, skinned and
  boned
1 eating apple, peeled, cored and cut
  into chunks
⅔ cup ricotta
pinch paprika or curry powder
salt and black pepper
apple slices, to garnish

For the curried dippers
4 slices white bread, crusts removed
2 tbsp butter, softened
1 tsp curry paste

1 Place the smoked mackerel in a food processor with the apple, ricotta and seasonings.

2 Blend for about 2 minutes or until the mixture is really smooth. Check the seasoning, transfer to a small serving dish and chill.

3 Preheat the oven to 400°F. To make the curried dippers, place the bread on a baking sheet. Blend the butter and curry paste thoroughly, then spread over the bread.

4 Cook the bread in the oven for about 10 minutes, or until crisp and golden. Cut into fingers and serve, while still warm, with the dip, garnished with the apple slices.

> **COOK'S TIP**
> Instead of using plain sliced bread, try other breads for the dippers – Italian ciabatta, rye, or pita breads would be excellent.

MUSHROOM POPOVERS

Children usually love traditional Yorkshire puddings, so don't just serve them with roasts. Here is a quick mushroom filling, though leftover roast meat, chopped up with gravy, is also good.

INGREDIENTS

Serves 4
1 egg
1 cup flour
1¼ cups milk
pinch salt

For the filling
1 tbsp sunflower oil
4oz mushrooms, sliced
few drops lemon juice
2 tsp chopped fresh parsley or thyme
¼ red bell pepper, seeded and chopped
salt and black pepper
fresh basil leaves, to garnish

1 To make the popovers, whisk the egg and flour together and gradually add a little milk to blend, then whisk in the rest of the milk to make a smooth batter. Add a pinch of salt and leave the batter to stand for 10–20 minutes.

2 When required, preheat the oven to 425°F. Pour very little oil into the base of eight popover pans and heat through in the oven for 4–5 minutes. Pour the batter into the very hot pans and cook for 20 minutes or until well risen and crispy.

3 Meanwhile, make the filling; heat the oil and sauté the mushrooms with the lemon juice, herbs and seasoning until most of their liquid has evaporated. Add the bell pepper at the last minute so that it keeps its crunch. Season to taste.

4 To serve, spoon the filling into the hot popover shells and scatter over the basil leaves.

Tomato and Garlic Stuffed Muffins

Ingredients

Serves 4

4 muffins
2 tbsp garlic butter, softened
2 medium tomatoes
8 small pieces mozzarella or Edam
  cheese
salt and black pepper

1 Preheat the oven to 375°F. Cut the muffins almost, but not completely, in halves horizontally.

2 Spread each half with a little garlic butter. Slice the tomatoes and arrange on the bases, then sprinkle with seasoning to taste.

3 Slide the slices of mozzarella or Edam cheese on top of the tomatoes, then close the muffins neatly and wrap in foil. Put the parcels on a baking sheet and bake for 20 minutes.

4 Serve the muffins hot with a selection of tangy chutneys and pickles, if you like.

Freezer Note
Prepare the filled muffins and freeze them, wrapped, ready to heat through from frozen.

Tuna Croissants

For an unusual packed lunch or picnic, these croissants are delicious. They will keep moist for several hours, well wrapped. Or they can be warmed through in the oven to serve immediately.

Ingredients

Serves 4

4 large fresh croissants
¾ cup canned tuna
½ cup canned corn
2 tbsp mayonnaise
8 crisp lettuce leaves
2 tomatoes, sliced
2 tbsp chopped green olives
salt and black pepper

1 Split the croissants in half horizontally and then warm them through in the oven, if you wish.

2 Place the tuna, corn and mayonnaise in a small bowl and mix well. Tear the lettuce into large pieces and arrange on the bottom halves of the croissants, then add the tomato slices.

3 Spoon the tuna and sweetcorn mixture over the tomatoes and scatter over the olives. Sprinkle with seasoning to taste, then replace the croissant tops and serve at once.

Cook's Tip
Use chopped boiled eggs, peeled shrimp, cooked chicken or bacon, mixed with a little mayonnaise, in place of the tuna, if you like.

CHICORY WITH CHEESE AND PEPPERS

Calorie counters can tuck into this crunchy treat. Serve as a starter, with salad for a light lunch, or as finger food.

— INGREDIENTS —

Makes about 16

2 large heads of chicory
½ cup low fat cream or curd cheese
1 tbsp thick plain yogurt
1 garlic clove, crushed
2 tbsp chopped sun-dried
* tomatoes, preserved in oil, drained*
2 tbsp seeded and chopped red
* pepper*
1 tbsp snipped fresh chives
1 tbsp chopped fresh basil
salt and black pepper
shredded red bell pepper, to garnish

1 Trim the chicory and carefully separate the leaves. Arrange on a large platter or serving dish.

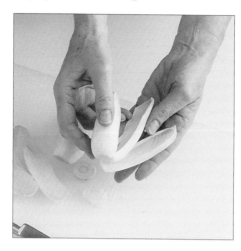

2 Blend or beat together the cheese, yogurt and garlic. Add the tomato, pepper and herbs, and season to taste.

3 Put a teaspoonful of the filling in each chicory leaf, at the stalk end, and garnish with the shredded pepper.

> COOK'S TIP
> Celery would be just as good if chicory is not available.

CHICKEN AND AVOCADO MAYONNAISE

You need quite firm 'scoops' or forks to eat this starter, so don't be tempted to try to pass it round as finger food.

— INGREDIENTS —

Serves 4

2 tbsp mayonnaise
1 tbsp ricotta
2 garlic cloves, crushed
1 cup chopped cooked chicken
1 large ripe, but firm, avocado, peeled
* and pitted*
2 tbsp lemon juice
salt and black pepper
nacho chips or tortilla chips, to serve

1 Mix together the mayonnaise, ricotta, garlic, and seasoning to taste, in a small bowl. Stir in the chopped chicken.

2 Chop the avocado and immediately toss in lemon juice, then mix gently into the chicken mixture. Check the seasoning and chill until required.

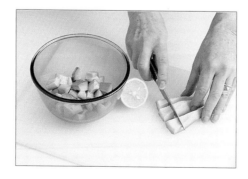

3 Serve in small serving dishes with the chips as scoops.

> COOK'S TIP
> This mixture also makes a great, chunky filling for sandwiches, baps or pita bread. Or serve as a main course salad, heaped on to a base of mixed salad leaves.

MEAT DISHES

It is well known today that we would be better off eating less meat. This doesn't mean we need to cut out the good old favorites, just eat a smaller portion with a greater variety of vegetables. When buying meat, be sure you get the cut you really want. If in doubt, whether you are in a butcher's shop or a supermarket, ask for advice. There is excellent quality meat available for the occasions when you want to splurge and a large choice of more economical yet tasty cuts to choose from, too. Never accept poor quality for the sake of cheapness. Included here are some very quick-to-cook ideas for mid-week meals, such as Spiced Pork with Creamy Mushrooms, and Lamb's Liver with Peppers, as well as several delicious dishes that can be prepared and cooked ahead.

OXTAIL BRAISED IN RED WINE

Always plan to cook oxtail 1–2 days before you wish to eat it. This gives you time to skim off the fat before serving.

Serves 3–4

4 tbsp sunflower oil
1 oxtail (about 2¼ lb), cut in pieces
2 onions
2 carrots, quartered
2 celery stalks, cut in pieces
1¼ cups beef stock
1¼ cups red wine
bouquet garni
1 tbsp flour
8oz can chopped tomatoes
salt and black pepper
1 tbsp chopped fresh parsley, to garnish

1 Heat half the oil in a large flameproof casserole or ovenproof pan with a tight-fitting lid. Sauté the pieces of oxtail until well browned.

2 Preheat the oven to 325°F. Add one of the onions, sliced, the pieces of carrot and celery, the stock, wine, bouquet garni, and seasoning. Bring to a boil and then cook in the oven for 1 hour.

3 Baste and stir well, reduce the oven temperature to 300°F for 1½–2 hours, or until the meat is very tender. Remove from the oven.

4 Leave to cool completely, then discard the surface fat and reheat. Remove the oxtail and reserve. Strain the stock; discard the vegetables. Preheat the oven to 350°F.

5 Fry the remaining onion, sliced, with the remaining oil in a large pan until golden. Stir in the flour and cook, stirring, until turning golden.

6 Gradually stir in the stock, a little at a time as it thickens. Bring back to the boil and then stir in the tomatoes. Add the oxtail, and seasoning to taste. Cover and cook in the oven for 30 minutes, or until the oxtail is heated through and really tender. Serve hot, sprinkled with the fresh parsley.

BRAISED BRISKET WITH DUMPLINGS

Brisket is very underrated and most often eaten as salt beef or pastrami these days. Given plenty of gentle cooking it produces a deliciously tender pot roast for eating hot with dumplings, or to serve cold with baked potatoes and salad.

INGREDIENTS

Serves 6–8
1 tbsp sunflower oil
2 onions, sliced
2 lb piece of rolled brisket, tied
1¼ cups hot beef stock
1¼ cups beer
2 bay leaves
few parsley stalks
2 parsnips, chopped
2 carrots, sliced
½ rutabaga, chopped

For the dumplings
2 tbsp butter
1½ cups self-rising flour, sifted
1 tsp dry mustard
1 tsp each dried sage, thyme and
	parsley
salt and black pepper
fresh herb sprigs, such as parsley,
	oregano or thyme, to garnish

1 Preheat the oven to 325°F. Heat the oil in a large flameproof casserole or ovenproof pan and fry the onions until well browned.

2 Place the meat on top, then add the hot stock, the beer, bay leaves and parsley stalks and bring to the boil. Cover and transfer to the oven for 2 hours, basting occasionally.

3 Meanwhile, prepare the vegetables and make the dumplings. Rub the butter into the flour, then mix in the dry mustard, herbs and seasoning, and add sufficient water to mix to a soft dough mixture. Shape into about 12 small balls.

4 When the meat is just about tender, add the vegetables and cook for 20 minutes. Check the seasoning, add the dumplings and continue cooking for 15 minutes, until they are nicely swollen. Serve hot, garnished with herb sprigs.

SPICED SHOULDER OF LAMB

The stuffing here is really used as a flavoring rather than a way of making the meat go further.

INGREDIENTS

Serves 6–8
1 cup fresh white breadcrumbs
6 tbsp chopped, mixed fresh herbs, such as basil, chives and parsley
3 garlic cloves, crushed
2 tbsp lemon juice
1 large shoulder of lamb, (blade bone removed) about 4–4½ lb
1 tsp each ground turmeric, coriander, cinnamon and paprika
little olive oil
salt and black pepper
fresh rosemary, to garnish

1 Preheat the oven to 425°F. Mix the breadcrumbs, herbs, garlic and lemon juice thoroughly together. Add plenty of seasoning.

2 Place the lamb on a work surface and open out the cavity. Spoon the breadcrumb mixture inside the lamb, then tie the lamb securely with string to completely enclose the stuffing.

3 Mix the spices together with salt and pepper. Brush the lamb well with oil and then rub on the spice mixture. Bake for 20 minutes, then reduce the heat to 375°F for another 1½ hours. (If you prefer lamb well done, cook for another 15–30 minutes.) Leave to rest in a warm place for 15 minutes, then slice and serve hot.

PORK CHOPS WITH WALNUT BUTTER

There is no chance that your pork chops will be dry if you cook them this way.

INGREDIENTS

Serves 4
4 lean, or well trimmed, pork chops
2 oranges
4 tbsp butter, softened
1 tbsp snipped chives
½ cup finely chopped walnuts
salt and black pepper

1 Preheat the oven to 400°F. Sprinkle the chops with seasoning to taste and place them in one layer in a shallow baking dish.

2 Grate the rind of one orange into a bowl, add the juice of half of one of the oranges, the butter, chives, walnuts and seasoning to taste.

3 Beat the flavored butter until soft, then spread over one side of the chops. Bake the chops for 15 minutes.

4 Meanwhile, peel the remaining half and whole orange, removing all the white pith, then cut into thin slices.

5 Baste the chops with the walnut butter, and then cook the chops for another 5 minutes if necessary, or serve immediately with the orange slices and a salad of lamb's lettuce and chicory, and new potatoes.

COOK'S TIP
Use finely chopped pecans or other nuts in place of the walnuts, if you prefer. You could also substitute lemons for the oranges.

LAMB STEAKS WITH MINTY DRESSING

INGREDIENTS

Serves 4

4 shoulder steaks of lamb
1 large garlic clove, crushed
½ in piece of ginger root, grated
10–12 coriander seeds, crushed
⅔ cup plain yogurt
2 tbsp olive oil
1 tsp walnut or sesame oil
1 tbsp orange juice
2 tbsp chopped fresh mint
½ green bell pepper, seeded and finely
   shredded
1 small red onion, thinly sliced
½ head oak leaf lettuce, torn into small
   pieces
salt and black pepper

1 Place the steaks on a flat dish or tray. Pound together, or crush, the garlic, ginger and coriander seeds, then mix in half the yogurt and seasoning. Spread over the meat and leave for 1–2 hours, turning once.

2 Remove the steaks and scrape off the marinade. Wipe the steaks dry and then brush with a little olive oil and sprinkle with seasoning. Grill or barbecue until as pink, or as well done as you wish.

3 Whisk the remaining olive oil and the walnut or sesame oil into the remaining yogurt with the orange juice, mint, and seasoning to taste. Add a little water if it is too thick for your taste. Toss the pepper, onion and lettuce together lightly.

4 Serve the grilled steaks at once with the tossed salad and the yogurt and mint dressing.

> **COOK'S TIP**
> Lamb shoulder steaks are the best value for this dish, but not always available – you could use leg steaks or chops instead.

GROUND BEEF PIE WITH GARLIC POTATOES

This is almost a complete meal in itself, but you could add lots more vegetables to the meat to make it go further.

INGREDIENTS

Serves 4
1 lb lean ground beef
1 onion, chopped
3 carrots, sliced
4 tomatoes, peeled and chopped
1¼ cups beef stock
1 tsp cornstarch
1 tbsp chopped, mixed herbs,
   or 1 tsp dried
2 tbsp olive oil
2 garlic cloves, crushed
1¼ lb potatoes (3 large), par-cooked
   and sliced
salt and black pepper

1 Preheat the oven to 350°F. Stir-fry the meat and onion in a large pan until browned. Add the carrots and tomatoes to the pan.

2 Stir in the stock, with the cornstarch blended in, and the herbs. Bring to a boil and simmer for 2–3 minutes, then season to taste. Transfer to a shallow ovenproof dish.

3 Mix the oil, garlic and seasoning together. Layer the potatoes on top of the meat mixture, brushing liberally with the garlic oil. Cook for 30–40 minutes, until the potatoes are tender and golden. Serve with a green salad and crisp green beans or snow peas.

COOK'S TIP
Leave the potatoes unpeeled, if you prefer, in this recipe, and incorporate other par-boiled root vegetables such as carrot, celeriac, rutabaga or turnip, and layer them with the potatoes.

EASY HAM LOAF

INGREDIENTS

Serves 8–10

1½ lb lean unsmoked bacon
1 onion, quartered
2 large garlic cloves
12oz breakfast sausage
3 cups fresh breadcrumbs
2 tbsp chopped, mixed fresh herbs,
    or 2 tsp dried
2 tsp grated orange rind
1 egg
salt and black pepper

For the sauce

4 tomatoes, peeled, seeded and
    chopped
1 shallot, chopped
4 tbsp fresh orange juice
2 tsp balsamic or sherry vinegar
2 tsp olive oil
1 tbsp chopped fresh basil
few basil leaves, to garnish

1 Preheat the oven to 350°F. Finely chop the bacon, onion and garlic in a food processor, then mix in the rest of the ingredients until well blended. Season to taste.

2 Pack into a 2 lb loaf pan. Cover with wax paper and bake for 1½ hours, or until firm.

3 Meanwhile, make the sauce; simmer the tomatoes, shallot, orange juice, vinegar, olive oil and chopped fresh basil for 10–12 minutes, stirring occasionally. Add seasoning, to taste.

4 Serve the ham loaf hot or cold, with the tomato sauce, and accompanied by new potatoes and broccoli.

LAMBURGERS WITH MELTING CENTERS

Try these lamb-based hamburgers on the children, for a change, but keep them quite small. You can prepare them in advance and freeze them, between sheets of wax paper.

INGREDIENTS

Makes 6

1 lb ground lamb
few drops Worcestershire sauce
pinch dried marjoram
2oz Bel Paese, feta or other tasty, but
    not strong cheese, diced
salt and black pepper
little olive oil

1 Place the ground lamb in a bowl with the Worcestershire sauce, marjoram, and seasoning to taste and mix thoroughly.

2 Divide the mixture into six and push a little of the diced cheese into the middle of each one. Mold the lamb around the cheese, shape into hamburgers and leave to stand for 10–20 minutes.

3 Brush the grill pan and the burgers lightly with oil and grill under a high heat, for 3–5 minutes on each side, or until cooked to your taste.

4 Serve the lamburgers with Italian bread and a salad.

GLAZED HAM WITH SPICED PEACHES

One of the most pleasing things about today's hams is there is so little waste. They're easy to cook, can be served hot or cold, and make great leftovers.

INGREDIENTS

Serves 6
3–3½ lb fresh or smoked ham
2½ cups cider
1 tbsp ground cinnamon
few black peppercorns, crushed
4–6 tbsp red currant jelly
15oz can peach slices in fruit juice
1 tsp mixed spice
1 tbsp cider vinegar
sprigs of rosemary

1 If you prefer a smoked ham, be sure to soak it for at least 2 hours, or overnight first. Drain well.

2 Place the ham in a large pan with the cider, and add fresh water to cover. Add the cinnamon and peppercorns. Bring to a boil and simmer until cooked, allowing 20 minutes per 1 lb and about 20 minutes over.

3 Preheat the oven to 400°F. Drain (saving the liquid), cool slightly, then cut away the skin neatly with a sharp knife. Score the fat, in diamonds, then coat with 2–4 tbsp of the red currant jelly. Transfer to a roasting pan and bake for 10 minutes until golden brown.

4 Meanwhile, make the spiced peaches; place ⅔ cup of the ham cooking liquid in a pan with the peach juice, the mixed spice, vinegar and 2 tbsp red currant jelly. Simmer for 10–15 minutes until syrupy. Add the peach slices and heat through. Serve hot with the ham, garnished with rosemary.

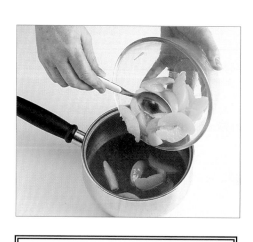

> COOK'S TIP
> If you want a quicker serving accompaniment, choose a tasty fruit chutney, or buy ready-made spiced peaches or pears.

SPICED PORK WITH CREAMY MUSHROOMS

This is incredibly quick and very easy, too. Also it looks – and tastes – good enough to serve to last-minute guests.

INGREDIENTS

Serves 4

1–1¼ lb pork fillet or tenderloin
little olive oil
1 tsp dried chopped garlic
finely grated rind of ½ lemon
2 tsp Cajun seasoning mix
½ in piece of ginger root, grated
4oz mushrooms, sliced
1–2 tbsp crème fraîche
2 tbsp dry white wine
salt and black pepper

1 Preheat the oven to 450°F. Lightly oil a sheet of foil, just large enough to enclose the meat. Place the meat on the foil, on a baking sheet, and brush with olive oil.

2 Sprinkle all the seasonings evenly over the meat. Wrap the meat very tightly in the foil and cook in the oven for 15 minutes.

3 Reduce the heat to 375°F and cook for a further 10–15 minutes or until the pork is really tender. (Don't open up the foil too often.)

4 Meanwhile, cook the mushrooms in a separate pan in very little olive oil, tossing them occasionally, until tender. When the pork is ready, open up the foil and carefully pour the juices into the mushroom pan.

5 Blend the crème fraîche, wine, and seasoning to taste into the mushroom mixture. Cook over low heat for only 1–2 minutes while carving the pork into neat slices.

6 Serve the pork at once with the creamy mushroom sauce.

COOK'S TIP
Instead of Cajun seasoning mix, which is both hot and herby, use a few drops Tabasco sauce, 1 tsp dried mixed herbs and a shake of ground coriander, cardamom and paprika.

Ragoût of Veal

If you are looking for a low calorie dish to treat yourself – or some guests – then this is perfect, and quick, too.

INGREDIENTS

Serves 4

1 lb veal fillet or loin
2 tbsp olive oil
10–12 pearl onions, kept whole
1 yellow pepper, seeded and cut
*   in eight*
1 orange or red bell pepper, seeded and
*   cut in eight*
3 plum tomatoes, peeled and quartered
4 sprigs of fresh basil
2 tbsp dry martini or sherry
salt and black pepper

1 Trim off any fat and cut the veal into cubes. Heat the oil in a frying pan and gently stir-fry the veal and onions until browned.

2 After a couple of minutes add the peppers and tomatoes. Continue stir-frying for another 4–5 minutes.

3 Add half the basil leaves, coarsely chopped (keep some for garnish), the martini or sherry, and seasoning. Cook, stirring frequently, for another 10 minutes, or until the meat is tender.

4 Sprinkle with the remaining basil leaves and serve hot.

Lamb's Liver with Peppers

If you really want to make a splash for a special occasion, then use sliced calves' liver instead of the lamb's.

INGREDIENTS

Serves 4

2 tbsp olive oil
2 shallots, sliced
1lb lamb's liver, cut in thin strips
1 garlic clove, crushed
2 tsp green peppercorns, crushed
*   (or more to taste)*
½ red pepper, seeded and cut in strips
½ orange or yellow bell pepper, seeded
*   and cut in strips*
2 tbsp crème fraîche or sour cream
salt and black pepper
rice or noodles, to serve

1 Heat the oil and fry the shallots briskly for 1 minute. Add the liver, garlic, peppercorns and peppers, then stir-fry for 3–4 minutes, or until no pink runs from the liver.

2 Stir in the crème fraîche or cream, season to taste and serve immediately with noodles or rice.

COOK'S TIP
Lamb's liver is best when still very slightly pink in the middle, although many prefer it well cooked. With this recipe you could please everyone, but do watch closely as it soon overcooks.

COCONUT BEEF CURRY

INGREDIENTS

Serves 4

1 lb rump steak, cubed
¾ cup unsweetened coconut
1¼ cups milk
1 tbsp soy sauce
2 tbsp vinegar
1 tbsp oil
2 garlic cloves, crushed
1 large onion, quartered
1 tsp each chili powder, ground
  cilantro, turmeric and ginger
salt and black pepper
fresh cilantro, to garnish

1 Place the beef in a shallow dish. Mix together the coconut and milk and bring almost to the boil. Cool slightly, then blend or process, or pound. Add the soy sauce and vinegar and pour over the beef. Leave, stirring occasionally, for 3–4 hours or overnight.

2 Heat the oil in a flameproof casserole and fry the garlic and onion until golden. Stir in the spices and seasoning and fry for 2 minutes.

3 Cover and cook over a low heat for about 2 hours, or until the meat is tender, stirring once or twice. Serve with rice, garnished with cilantro.

COOK'S TIP
This Malaysian combination needs the coconut, use shredded, creamed or fresh – but do be sure that it is not sweetened.

PORK AND APPLE HOT POT

INGREDIENTS

Serves 4–6

1¼ lb sparerib pork chops
2 tbsp sunflower oil
1 large onion, sliced
3 celery stalks, chopped
1 tbsp chopped fresh sage,
  or 1 tsp dried
1 tbsp chopped fresh parsley
2 eating apples, peeled, cored and cut
  in thick wedges
⅔ cup apple juice
⅔ cup stock
1 tbsp cornstarch
1 lb par-boiled, peeled potatoes
little melted butter
salt and black pepper
sprigs of sage, to garnish

1 Remove any bones from the pork and cut the meat into even-sized cubes. Sprinkle with seasoning.

2 Heat the oil in a pan and fry the onion and celery until golden. Remove and place half in the base of a casserole. Arrange the meat on top and sprinkle with half the herbs.

3 Add the apples and the rest of the onion, celery and herbs. Season to taste. Blend the apple juice with the stock and cornstarch and pour over.

4 Preheat the oven to 375°F. Top with the sliced potatoes and brush with melted butter. Cover and cook in the oven for 50–60 minutes, removing the lid for the last 15 minutes to brown the potatoes. Serve hot, garnished with sage.

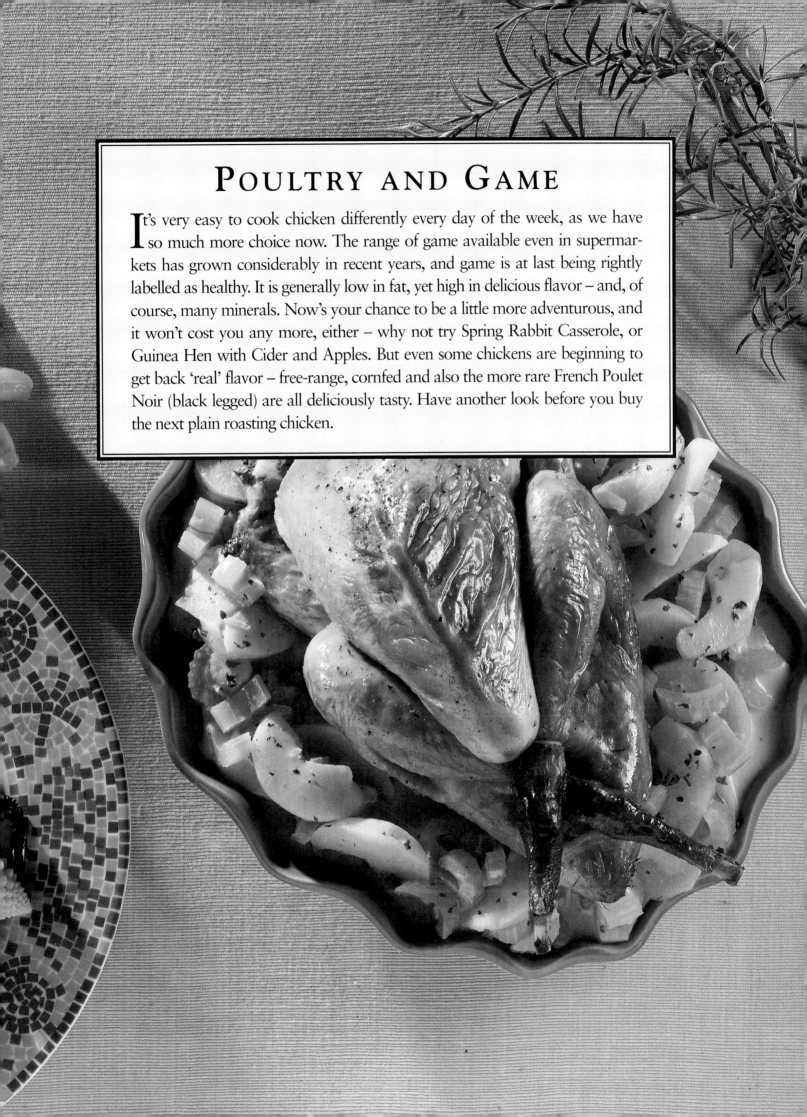

POULTRY AND GAME

It's very easy to cook chicken differently every day of the week, as we have so much more choice now. The range of game available even in supermarkets has grown considerably in recent years, and game is at last being rightly labelled as healthy. It is generally low in fat, yet high in delicious flavor – and, of course, many minerals. Now's your chance to be a little more adventurous, and it won't cost you any more, either – why not try Spring Rabbit Casserole, or Guinea Hen with Cider and Apples. But even some chickens are beginning to get back 'real' flavor – free-range, cornfed and also the more rare French Poulet Noir (black legged) are all deliciously tasty. Have another look before you buy the next plain roasting chicken.

CURRIED CHICKEN AND APRICOT PIE

This pie is unusually sweet-sour and very tasty. Use boneless turkey instead of chicken if you wish, or even some leftovers from a roast turkey – the dark, moist leg meat is best.

INGREDIENTS

Serves 6
2 tbsp sunflower oil
1 large onion, chopped
1 lb boneless chicken, roughly chopped
1 tbsp curry paste or powder
2 tbsp apricot or peach chutney
⅔ cup ready-to-eat dried apricots,
  halved
1 cup cooked, sliced carrots
1 tsp mixed dried herbs
4 tbsp crème fraîche or sour cream
12oz ready-made pie crust
little egg or milk, to glaze
salt and black pepper

1 Heat the oil in a large pan and fry the onion and chicken until just coloring. Add the curry paste or powder and fry for 2 minutes more.

2 Add the chutney, apricots, carrots, herbs and crème fraîche or cream to the pan with seasoning. Mix together well and then transfer to a deep 4–5 cup ovenproof pie dish.

3 Roll out the pastry to 1in wider than the pie dish. Cut a strip of pastry from the edge. Dampen the rim of the dish, press on the strip, then brush these strips with water and place the sheet of pastry on top. Press to seal.

4 Preheat the oven to 375°F. Trim off any excess pastry and use to make an attractive pattern on the top if you wish. Brush all over with beaten egg or milk and bake for 40 minutes, until crisp and golden.

CHICKEN WITH HERBS AND LENTILS

If your family doesn't like lentils (and some children don't), use rice instead.

INGREDIENTS

Serves 4

4oz piece of thick bacon or pork belly,
  rind removed, chopped
1 large onion, sliced
1¼ cups well-flavored chicken stock
bay leaf
2 sprigs each parsley, marjoram and
  thyme
2 cups green or brown lentils
4 chicken portions
salt and black pepper
2–4 tbsp garlic butter

1 Fry the bacon gently in a large, heavy-based flameproof casserole until all the fat runs out and the bacon begins to brown. Add the onions and fry for another 2 minutes.

2 Stir in the stock, bay leaf, herb stalks and some of the leafy parts (keep some herb sprigs for garnish), lentils and seasoning. Preheat the oven to 375°F.

3 Fry the chicken portions in a frying pan to brown the skin before placing on top of the lentils. Sprinkle with seasoning and some of the herbs.

4 Cover the casserole and cook in the oven for about 40 minutes. Serve with a tablespoon of garlic butter on each portion and a few of the remaining herb sprigs scattered over.

> **COOK'S TIP**
> For economy buy a smallish chicken and cut it in quarters, to give you four good portions.

CHICKEN WITH HONEY AND GRAPEFRUIT

Chicken breast portions cook very quickly and are ideal for suppers 'on-the-run' - but don't be tempted to overcook them. You could substitute boneless turkey steaks, or duck breast fillets for the chicken, if you like.

INGREDIENTS

Serves 4
4 chicken breast portions, skinned
3–4 tbsp honey
1 pink grapefruit, peeled and cut into 12 segments
salt and black pepper
three-coloured noodles and salad leaves, to serve

1 Make three quite deep, diagonal slits in the chicken flesh using a large sharp knife.

2 Brush the chicken with honey, and season. Preheat broiler.

3 Place the chicken in a flameproof dish, uncut side uppermost, under a medium broiler for 2–3 minutes, then turn over and place the grapefruit segments in the slits. Brush with more honey and cook for 5 minutes, or until tender.

4 If necessary, reduce the heat so that the honey glazed parts don't burn. Serve at once with three-coloured noodles and salad leaves.

CRISPY CHICKEN WITH GARLICKY RICE

Chicken wings cooked until they are really tender have a surprising amount of meat on them, and make a very economical supper for a crowd of youngsters – provide lots of kitchen paper or napkins for the sticky fingers.

INGREDIENTS

Serves 4
1 large onion, chopped
2 garlic cloves, crushed
2 tbsp sunflower oil
⅞ cup patna or basmati rice
1½ cups hot chicken stock
2 tsp finely grated lemon rind
2 tbsp chopped mixed herbs
8 or 12 chicken wings
½ cup flour
salt and black pepper

1 Preheat the oven to 400°F. Fry the onion and garlic in the oil in a large ovenproof pan until golden. Add the patna or basmati rice and toss until well coated in oil.

2 Stir in the stock, lemon rind and herbs and bring to a boil. Cover and cook in the middle of the oven for 40–50 minutes. Stir the rice once or twice during cooking.

3 Meanwhile, wipe dry the chicken wings. Season the flour and use to coat the chicken portions thoroughly, dusting off any excess.

4 Place the chicken wings in a small roasting pan and cook in the top of the oven for 30–40 minutes, turning once, until crispy and golden.

5 Serve the rice and the crispy chicken wings together with a fresh tomato sauce and a selection of vegetables.

THAI CHICKEN AND VEGETABLE STIR-FRY

INGREDIENTS

Serves 4

1 piece lemon grass (or the rind of ½ lemon)

½in piece of fresh ginger root

1 large garlic clove, chopped

2 tbsp sunflower oil

10oz lean chicken, thinly sliced

½ red pepper, seeded and sliced

½ green pepper, seeded and sliced

4 scallions, chopped

2 medium carrots, cut into matchsticks

4oz fine green beans

2 tbsp oyster sauce

pinch sugar

salt and black pepper

¼ cup salted peanuts, lightly crushed, and cilantro leaves, to garnish

1 Thinly slice the lemon grass or lemon rind. Peel and chop the ginger and garlic. Heat the oil in a frying pan over a high heat until hazy. Add the lemon grass or lemon rind, ginger and garlic, and stir-fry for 30 seconds until brown.

2 Add the chicken and stir-fry for 2 minutes. Then add the vegetables and stir-fry for 4–5 minutes, until the chicken is cooked and the vegetables are almost cooked.

3 Finally stir in the oyster sauce, sugar and seasoning to taste and stir-fry for another minute to mix and blend well. Serve at once, sprinkled with the peanuts and cilantro leaves and accompanied with rice.

COOK'S TIP
Make this quick supper dish a little hotter by adding more fresh ginger root, if you wish.

TURKEY WITH YELLOW PEPPER SAUCE

──── INGREDIENTS ────

Serves 4

2 tbsp olive oil

2 large yellow bell peppers, seeded and
  chopped

1 small onion, chopped

1 tbsp freshly squeezed orange juice

1¼ cups chicken stock

4 turkey escalopes

3oz Boursin or garlicky cream cheese

12 fresh basil leaves

2 tbsp butter

salt and black pepper

1 To make the yellow pepper sauce;
heat half the oil in a pan and gently
fry the peppers and onion until beginning to soften. Add the orange juice
and stock and cook until very soft.

2 Meanwhile, lay the turkey escalopes
out flat and pound them out lightly.

3 Spread the turkey escalopes with the
Boursin or garlicky cream cheese.
Chop half the basil and sprinkle on top,
then roll up, tucking in the ends like an
envelope, and secure neatly with half a
toothpick.

4 Heat the remaining oil and the butter in a frying pan and fry the
escalopes for 7–8 minutes, turning them
frequently, until golden and cooked.

5 While the escalopes are cooking,
press the pepper mixture through a
sieve, or blend until smooth, then strain
back into the pan. Season to taste and
warm through, or serve cold, with the
escalopes, garnished with the remaining
basil leaves.

COOK'S TIP
Chicken breast fillets or veal
escalopes could be used in place
of the turkey, if you prefer.

CHICKEN, CARROT AND LEEK PARCELS

These intriguing parcels may sound a bit fussy for everyday, but they take very little time and you can freeze them – ready to cook gently from frozen.

INGREDIENTS

Serves 4
4 *chicken fillets or boneless breast*
  portions
2 *small leeks, sliced*
2 *carrots, grated*
4 *pitted black olives, chopped*
1 *garlic clove, crushed*
1–2 *tbsp olive oil*
8 *anchovy fillets*
salt and black pepper
black olives and herb sprigs, to garnish

1 Preheat the oven to 400°F. Season the chicken well.

2 Divide the leeks equally among four sheets of greased wax paper, about 9in square. Place a piece of chicken on top of each.

3 Mix the carrots, olives, garlic and oil together. Season lightly and place on top of the chicken portions. Top each with two of the anchovy fillets, then carefully wrap up each parcel, making sure the paper folds are underneath and the carrot mixture on top.

4 Bake for 20 minutes and serve hot, in the paper, garnished with black olives and herb sprigs.

CHICKEN IN A TOMATO COAT

INGREDIENTS

Serves 4–6
3½– 4 *lb free-range chicken*
1 *small onion*
1 *tbsp butter*
5 *tbsp ready-made tomato sauce*
2 *tbsp chopped, mixed fresh herbs,*
  such as parsley, tarragon, sage, basil
  and marjoram, or 2 tsp dried
small glass of dry white wine
2–3 *small tomatoes, sliced*
olive oil
little cornstarch (optional)
salt and black pepper

1 Preheat the oven to 375°F. Wash and wipe dry the chicken and place in a roasting pan. Place the onion, butter and some seasoning inside the chicken.

2 Spread most of the tomato sauce over the chicken and sprinkle with half the herbs and some seasoning. Pour the wine into the roasting pan.

3 Cover with foil, then roast for 1½ hours, basting occasionally. Remove the foil, spread with the remaining sauce and the sliced tomatoes and drizzle with oil. Continue cooking for a further 20–30 minutes, or until the chicken is cooked through.

4 Sprinkle the remaining herbs over the chicken, then carve into portions. Thicken the sauce with a little cornstarch if you wish. Serve hot.

MIXED GAME PIE

Serves 4

*1 lb game meat, off the bone (plus the
   carcasses and bones)*

1 small onion, halved

2 bay leaves

2 carrots, halved

few black peppercorns

1 tbsp oil

*3oz bacon pieces, rinded and
   chopped*

1 tbsp flour

3 tbsp sweet sherry or Madeira

2 tsp ground ginger

grated rind and juice of ½ orange

12oz ready-made puff pastry

egg or milk, to glaze

salt and black pepper

1 Place the carcasses and bones in a pan, with any giblets and half the onion, the bay leaves, carrots and black peppercorns. Cover with water and bring to the boil. Simmer until reduced to about 1¼ cups, then strain the stock, ready to use.

2 Cut the game meat into even size pieces. Fry the remaining onion, chopped, in the oil until softened. Then add the bacon and meat and fry quickly to seal. Sprinkle on the flour and stir until beginning to brown. Gradually add the stock, stirring as it thickens, then add the sherry or Madeira, ginger, orange rind and juice, and seasoning. Simmer for 20 minutes.

3 Transfer to a 3¾ cup pie dish and allow to cool slightly. Put a pie funnel in the centre of the filling to help hold up the pastry.

4 Preheat the oven to 425°F. Roll out the pastry to 1in larger than the dish. Cut off a ½ in strip all round. Dampen the rim of the dish and press on the strip of pastry. Dampen again and then lift the pastry carefully over the pie, sealing the edges well at the rim. Trim off the excess pastry, use to decorate the top, then brush the pie with egg or milk.

5 Bake for 15 minutes, then reduce the heat to 375°F, for a further 25–30 minutes. Serve with red currant, or sage and apple, jelly.

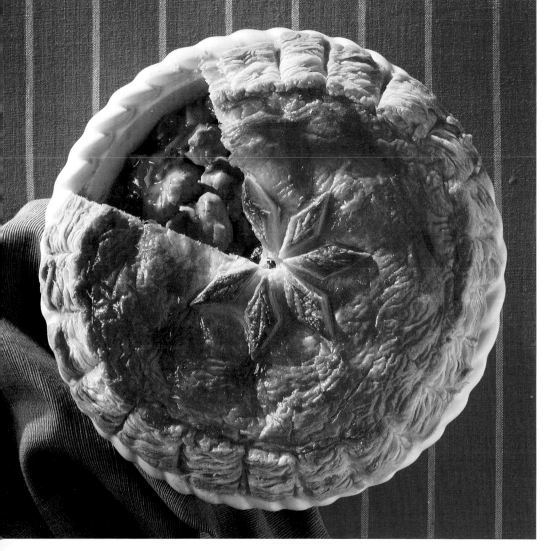

GUINEA HEN WITH CIDER AND APPLES

Guinea hens are farmed, so they are available quite frequently in supermarkets, usually fresh. Their flavor is reminiscent of an old-fashioned chicken – not really gamey, but they do have slightly darker meat.

INGREDIENTS

Serves 4–6
4–4½ lb guinea hen
1 onion, halved
3 celery stalks
3 bay leaves
little butter
1¼ cups dry cider
⅔ cup chicken stock
2 small apples, peeled and sliced
4 tbsp thick heavy cream
few sage leaves
2 tbsp chopped fresh parsley
salt and black pepper

1 If the guinea hen is packed with its giblets, put them in a pan with water to cover, half the onion, a stalk of celery, a bay leaf and seasoning. Simmer for 30 minutes, or until you have about ⅔ cup well-flavored stock.

2 Preheat the oven to 375°F. Wash and wipe dry the bird and place the remaining onion half and a tablespoon of butter inside the body cavity. Place in a roasting dish, sprinkle with seasoning to taste, and dot with a few tablespoons of butter.

3 Pour the cider and chicken stock into the dish and cover with a lid or foil. Bake for 25 minutes per 1 lb, basting occasionally.

4 Uncover for the last 20 minutes, baste well again and add the prepared apples and the celery, sliced. When the guinea hen is cooked, transfer it to a warm serving dish and keep warm. Remove the apples and celery with a slotted spoon and set aside.

5 Boil the liquid rapidly to reduce to about ⅔ cup. Stir in the cream, seasoning to taste and the sage leaves, and cook for a few minutes more to reduce slightly. Return the apples to this pan with the parsley and warm through, then serve with or around the bird.

DUCK BREASTS WITH BLACKBERRIES

If there isn't any blackberry jelly in your kitchen cupboard, you could substitute red currant jelly instead.

INGREDIENTS

Serves 4

4 duck breasts
finely grated rind and juice of 1 orange
2 tbsp blackberry jelly
salt and black pepper

1 Heat a heavy-based frying pan and place the duck portions skin side down first. Fry for 3–4 minutes. Meanwhile, sprinkle the meat side with seasoning and the orange rind.

2 Turn the duck over and continue cooking for 3–4 minutes. Spread the skin side with some of the blackberry jelly while cooking, and pour the orange juice over the portions.

3 Spread a little more jelly over the duck breasts, then turn them over and cook for 1–2 minutes more, until just cooked, but still slightly pink in the middle. Serve the duck breasts with the glaze poured over, accompanied by new potatoes and a watercress and orange salad.

SPRING RABBIT CASSEROLE

If you have never tried rabbit before, you will find it very similar to chicken, but with just a slightly sweeter taste. You could replace the rabbit with chicken in this recipe, if you prefer – cook it in exactly the same way.

INGREDIENTS

Serves 4

1 tbsp sunflower oil
1 lb boneless rabbit
4 rashers bacon, rinded and chopped
2 leeks, sliced
4 scallions, sliced
3 celery stalks, chopped
4 small carrots, sliced
1¼ cups vegetable stock
2 tsp Dijon mustard
1 tsp grated lemon rind
3–4 tbsp crème fraîche or sour cream
salt and black pepper
herby mashed potatoes, to serve

1 Heat the oil in a large flameproof casserole and fry the rabbit pieces until browned all over. Preheat the oven to 375°F.

2 Add the bacon and vegetables and toss over the heat for 1 minute. Add the stock, mustard, lemon rind and crème fraîche or sour cream, and seasoning to taste, then bring to the boil.

3 Cover and cook for 35–40 minutes, or until the rabbit is tender (it should take no longer than chicken). Serve with herby mashed potatoes – creamed potatoes well flavored and colored with chopped fresh parsley and snipped chives.

TURKEY STRIPS WITH SOUR CREAM DIP

INGREDIENTS

Serves 4

12oz turkey fillets, or 2 boneless breast
    portions
1 cup fine fresh breadcrumbs
¼ tsp paprika
1 egg, lightly beaten
3 tbsp sour cream
1 tbsp ready-made tomato sauce
1 tbsp mayonnaise
salt and black pepper

1 Preheat the oven to 375°F. Cut the
turkey into strips. Mix the breadcrumbs with paprika and season with
salt and pepper.

2 Dip the turkey into the egg, then
into the breadcrumbs, until thoroughly and evenly coated. Place on a
baking sheet when they are prepared.

3 Cook the turkey in the top of the
oven for 20 minutes, until crisp and
golden. Turn once during cooking.

4 To make the dip; mix the sour
cream, tomato sauce and mayonnaise together in a small bowl and
season to taste. Serve the turkey strips
with baked potatoes and a green salad
or crisp green vegetables, accompanied
by the dip.

CHICKEN, BACON AND CORN KABOBS

Don't wait for barbecue weather
to have kabobs. If you are serving them to children, remember
to remove the kabob sticks first.

INGREDIENTS

Serves 4

2 ears of corn, cooked
8 thick rashers bacon
8 brown cap mushrooms, halved
2 small chicken fillets
2 tbsp sunflower oil
1 tbsp lemon juice
1 tbsp maple syrup
salt and black pepper

1 Cook the corn in boiling water until
tender, then drain and cool. Stretch
the bacon rashers with the back of a
knife; cut each in half. Wrap a piece
around each half mushroom.

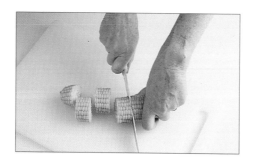

2 Cut both the corn and chicken into
eight equal pieces. Mix together the
oil, lemon juice, syrup and seasoning
and brush liberally over the chicken.

3 Thread the corn, bacon-wrapped
mushrooms and chicken pieces
alternately on skewers and brush all
over with the lemon dressing.

4 Broil the kabobs for 8–10 minutes,
turning them once and basting
occasionally with any extra dressing.
Serve hot with either a crisp green or
mixed leaf salad.

FISH AND SEAFOOD

Preparing fish so often puts people off cooking it, yet – with just a little planning or searching – this problem can be avoided. Fishmongers (given time, of course) will happily prepare the fish for you, and supermarkets now have almost everything ready-prepared. There are several dishes here which don't need any skilled preparation at all, such as Roast Cod with Mixed Beans, or Parmesan Fish Strips; and some which you will probably find surprisingly easy, once you try. For really speedy cooking you can't beat fish, whether it is the grilled Monkfish and Potato Kabobs, or Trout with Curried Orange Butter. And if you would like to be a little more adventurous, then you could either go California-style with mackerel, or try Swedish-style Gravadlax Trout.

GRAVADLAX TROUT

Although traditionally done with whole salmon, this marinating treatment also does wonders with small trout, but generally the larger the fish the better. If you ever get locally caught, large lake trout, this is the best thing to do with them.

INGREDIENTS

Serves 4
2 large trout, gutted and heads removed
1 bunch of dill

Marinade ingredients for each
1 lb of fish
½ tbsp coarse salt
½ tbsp sugar
½ tbsp crushed peppercorns

For the mustard sauce
1 tsp strong mustard
1 tbsp chopped fresh dill
2 tsp sugar
1 tsp cider vinegar
5 tbsp sour cream

1 Slit the trout from the stomach to the tail in a straight line, then lay each fish on its stomach, opened out, and press firmly along the backbone, down to the tail. Turn over and gently, with the point of a knife, ease out the whole of the backbone in one piece. Then pick out any other loose bones.

2 Weigh the fish now and calculate the quantities of marinade seasonings. Lay one fish skin side down in a tight-fitting, non-metallic dish. Wash and dry the dill and place on top.

3 Mix the marinade seasonings together and sprinkle evenly over the dill. Top with the other fish, cover with foil or a dish and place weights evenly on top of the fish.

4 Chill the fish for 48 hours. Turn every 6–12 hours, basting with the marinating liquid.

5 Mix all the sauce ingredients together and chill. Scrape away the dill and peppers from the fish and pat dry. Cut into fillets, or thinly slice the fish horizontally. Serve with hot bread and the mustard sauce.

PARMESAN FISH STRIPS

Use this batter, with or without the cheese, whenever you feel brave enough to fry fish. This is light and crisp, perfect with the tart cream sauce.

INGREDIENTS

Serves 4

12oz sole fillets, or thicker fish such as cod or haddock
little flour
oil, for deep-frying
salt and black pepper
sprigs of dill, to garnish

For the cream sauce
4 tbsp sour cream
4 tbsp mayonnaise
½ tsp grated lemon rind
2 tbsp chopped cornichons or capers
1 tbsp chopped, mixed fresh herbs, or 1 tsp dried

For the batter
¾ cup flour
¼ cup Parmesan cheese
1 tsp bicarbonate of soda
1 egg, separated
⅔ cup milk

1 To make the cream sauce, mix the sour cream, mayonnaise, lemon rind, cornichons or capers, herbs and seasoning together, then chill.

2 To make the batter, sift the flour into a bowl. Mix in the other dry ingredients and salt, and then whisk in the egg yolk and milk to give a thick yet smooth batter. Then gradually whisk in 6 tbsp water. Season and chill.

3 Skin the fish and cut into thin strips of similar length. Season the flour and then dip the fish lightly in the flour.

4 Heat at least 2in oil in a large pan with a lid. Whisk the egg white until stiff and gently fold into the batter until just blended.

5 Dip the floured fish into the batter, drain off any excess and then drop gently into the hot fat.

6 Cook the fish in batches so that the strips don't stick to one another, for only 3–4 minutes, turning once. When the batter is golden and crisp, remove the fish with a spatula. Place on wax paper on a plate in a warm oven while cooking the rest.

7 Serve hot with chips, or small baked potatoes, tomatoes and the cream sauce.

SEAFOOD SALAD PROVENÇALE

You can't beat this salad for an almost instant starter or main course, and it is perfect for a buffet table as it keeps so well.

INGREDIENTS

Serves 4

12oz mixed cooked seafood (shelled shrimp, mussels, clams, crabsticks)
2 tbsp ready-made tomato sauce
1 garlic clove, crushed
4 tbsp pimiento or mixed bell pepper antipasti
4 tbsp marinated artichokes
½ yellow bell pepper, seeded and sliced
lemon juice, to taste
2 tbsp white wine (optional)
salt and black pepper
2 tbsp chopped fresh parsley and whole shrimp, to garnish

1 Toss the seafood in the tomato sauce, add the garlic and leave for 5–10 minutes to absorb the flavors.

2 Mix together the pimiento or mixed bell pepper antipasti with the artichokes, the yellow bell pepper, lemon juice and wine, if using.

3 Stir in the seafood mixture, season to taste, and chill. Sprinkle with chopped parsley and garnish with whole shrimp before serving.

MONKFISH AND POTATO KABOBS

Monkfish is a good, firm fish, so it works well on kabobs and when cooked over a fierce heat.

INGREDIENTS

Serves 4

12–16 small new potatoes, cooked
12–16 seedless grapes
4in piece cucumber, peeled and cut in 8 pieces
10–12oz monkfish tail, boned and cubed
6 tbsp butter
grated rind and juice of 1 lime
1 tsp grated ginger root
1 tbsp chopped fresh parsley
3–4 tbsp white wine
salt and black pepper

1 Arrange the potatoes, grapes, cucumber and monkfish alternately on skewers.

2 Melt two-thirds of the butter and stir in the lime rind and juice, ginger, seasoning and half the parsley. Brush this all over the kabobs.

3 Preheat the broiler and cook the kabobs, in a dish or on a sheet of foil to catch all the juices, for 2 minutes on each side. Baste occasionally.

4 When cooked, transfer the kabobs to hot plates while heating the juices with the wine and the remaining butter. Check the seasoning, sprinkle the kabobs with parsley and serve with a salad and the tangy lime sauce.

SMOKED HADDOCK LYONNAISE

Serves 4

1 lb smoked cod or haddock
⅔ cup milk
2 onions, chopped
1 tbsp butter
1 tbsp cornstarch
⅔ cup Greek-style yogurt or ricotta
1 tsp ground turmeric
1 tsp paprika
4oz mushrooms, sliced
2 celery stalks, chopped
12oz firm cooked potatoes,
    preferably cold, diced
2 tbsp olive oil
½–1 cup soft white breadcrumbs
salt and black pepper

1 Poach the fish in the milk until just cooked. Remove the fish, reserving the liquid, then flake the fish and discard the skin and bones. Set aside.

2 Fry half the chopped onion in the butter until translucent. Stir in the cornstarch, then gradually blend in the fish cooking liquid and the yogurt and cook until thickened and smooth.

3 Stir in the turmeric, paprika, mushrooms and celery. Season to taste and add the flaked fish. Spoon into an ovenproof dish. Preheat the oven to 375°F.

4 Fry the remaining onion in the oil until translucent. Add the diced potatoes and stir until lightly coated in oil. Sprinkle on the breadcrumbs and seasoning.

5 Spoon this mixture over the fish and bake for 20–30 minutes, or until the top is nicely crisp and golden.

COOK'S TIP
Chopped cooked parsnips or turnips could also be used for the topping, but as with the potato, it is better if they are firm.

FISH JAMBALAYA

Jambalaya, from New Orleans, is not unlike a paella, but much more spicy. The name comes from the French word jambon, and tells us that the dish is based on ham, but you can add other ingredients of your choice, including fish and shellfish.

INGREDIENTS

Serves 4
2 tbsp oil
4oz smoked bacon, rinds removed, diced
1 onion, chopped
2 stalks celery, chopped
2 large garlic cloves, chopped
1 tsp cayenne pepper
2 bay leaves
1 tsp dried oregano
½ tsp dried thyme
4 tomatoes, peeled and chopped
⅔ cup ready-made tomato sauce
1¾ cups long grain rice
2 cups fish stock
6oz firm white fish (halibut, cod, scrod or haddock), skinned, boned and cubed
1 cup cooked, peeled shrimp
salt and black pepper
2 chopped scallions, to garnish

1 Heat the oil in a large saucepan and fry the bacon until crisp. Add the onion and celery and stir until beginning to stick on the base of the pan.

2 Add the garlic, cayenne pepper, herbs, tomatoes and seasoning and mix well. Stir in the tomato sauce, rice and stock and bring to the boil.

3 Preheat the oven to 350°F. Gently stir in the fish and transfer to an ovenproof dish. Cover tightly with foil and bake for 20–30 minutes, until the rice is just tender. Stir in the shrimp and heat through. Serve sprinkled with the scallions.

COOK'S TIP
A traditional and easy way to serve jambalaya is to fill an 8oz cup with the mixture and unmold it onto a hot plate. Then serve with Creole sauce (which you can buy ready-made) and garnish each portion with a whole shrimp.

SEARED SALMON WITH MINT SALSA

A little piece of salmon treated like this can go a surprisingly long way, with little or no effort. It is good with cod, too.

INGREDIENTS

Serves 4

2 large extra tasty tomatoes, peeled, seeded and diced
3in piece of cucumber, peeled and diced
1 tsp balsamic or red wine vinegar
2 tbsp chopped fresh mint, or 2 tsp dried
3 tbsp olive oil
4 salmon tail fillet pieces (about 1lb in all), or 1 tail piece which you will need to fillet yourself
2 tbsp butter
squeeze of lemon juice
salt and black pepper

1 To make the salsa, mix the tomatoes, cucumber, vinegar, mint and 1–2 tbsp olive oil together and season to taste. Chill.

2 Lay the fish between sheets of wax paper and gently bash with a rolling pin, to make them as flat as possible. Brush both sides with oil and season with salt and black pepper.

3 Heat half the butter in a non-stick frying pan and, when really hot, fry the fillets two at a time. Allow only about 1 minute each side and serve at once with a squeeze of lemon juice and the chilled salsa.

ROAST COD WITH MIXED BEANS

INGREDIENTS

Serves 4

4 thick cod steaks
3 tbsp sweet sherry or Madeira
14oz can spicy mixed beans, drained
14oz can kidney, borlotti or cannelini beans, drained
2 garlic cloves, crushed
1 tbsp olive oil
1 tsp grated orange rind
1 tbsp chopped fresh parsley
salt and black pepper

1 Skin the steaks, then pour over the sherry or Madeira and leave in a bowl, turning once, for 10 minutes.

2 Preheat the oven to 400°F. Mix the beans with the garlic and place in the base of an ovenproof dish. Place the fish on top and pour over the sherry or Madeira. Brush the fish with the oil, sprinkle with orange rind, half the parsley and seasoning.

3 Cover tightly with foil and cook for 15–20 minutes. Pierce the thickest part of the fish with a knife to check if it is cooked through and continue cooking for only another 2–3 minutes if necessary.

4 Baste the fish with a little of the juices which will have risen to the top of the beans. Then sprinkle with the rest of the parsley just before serving.

MUSSELS AND CLAMS IN TOMATO SAUCE

INGREDIENTS

Serves 4 as a starter or 2 as a main course

5 cups fresh mussels, scrubbed, bearded
   and well washed
2½ cups clams, well washed
⅔ cup white wine
1 tbsp olive oil
1 small onion, finely chopped
1 garlic clove, crushed
4 ripe medium tomatoes, peeled, seeded
   and chopped
1 tbsp chopped fresh parsley
1 tbsp chopped fresh basil or
   oregano
1 tsp orange rind
6 tbsp heavy cream
salt and black pepper
chopped fresh parsley, to garnish

1 Place the mussels and clams with the wine in a large pan, cover and bring to a boil. Cook for 2–3 minutes, or until all the shells open. Discard any clams and mussels which don't open. Drain out all the liquid, strain and reserve.

2 Heat the oil in a large pan and fry the onion and garlic for 2 minutes. Then add the tomatoes, herbs, orange rind and the fish liquid. Bring to the boil and cook for 4–5 minutes, until the tomatoes are cooked and the liquid reduced a little.

3 Add the cream and simmer for another couple of minutes. Season to taste. Pour this mixture over the mussels and clams and heat through well before serving with more parsley sprinkled over and plenty of hot bread for dipping into the sauce.

COOK'S TIP
Other small shellfish could be added to this dish – try cockles for instance, or add some shrimp or scallops with the cream in step 3.

FISH SOUFFLÉ WITH CHEESE TOPPING

This is an easy-going soufflé, which will not drop too much if kept waiting. On the other hand, it might be best to get the family seated before you take it out of the oven!

INGREDIENTS

Serves 4

12oz white fish, skinned and boned
⅔ cup milk
8oz cooked potatoes, still warm
1 garlic clove, crushed
2 eggs, separated
grated rind and juice of ½ small lemon
1 cup cooked, peeled shrimp
½ cup grated Cheddar cheese
salt and black pepper

1 Poach, or microwave, the fish in the milk until it flakes easily. Drain, reserving the milk, and place the fish in a bowl.

2 Mash the potatoes until really creamy, using as much of the fish milk as necessary. Then mash in the garlic, egg yolks, lemon rind and juice and seasoning to taste.

3 Preheat the oven to 425°F. Flake the fish and gently stir into the potato mixture with the shrimp. Season to taste.

4 Whisk the egg whites until stiff but not dry and gently fold them into the fish mixture. When smoothly blended, spoon into a greased gratin dish.

5 Sprinkle with the cheese and bake for 25–30 minutes, until the top is golden and just about firm to the touch. (If it browns too quickly, turn the temperature down to 400°F.)

> COOK'S TIP
> Smoked fish is also good for this soufflé, but as it has a stronger flavour, you could use less lemon and cheese.

TROUT WITH CURRIED ORANGE BUTTER

Small trout are perfect mid-week fare, and delicious served with this tangy butter. Children, particularly, like the mild curry flavour, but it is a good idea to fillet the cooked trout and remove the bones before serving this to very young children.

──────── INGREDIENTS ────────

Serves 4

2 tbsp butter, softened
1 tsp curry powder
1 tsp grated orange rind
4 small trout, gutted and heads
   removed
little oil
salt and black pepper
4 wedges of orange, to garnish

1 Mix the butter, curry powder, orange rind and seasoning together, wrap in foil and freeze for 10 minutes.

2 Brush the fish all over with oil and sprinkle well with seasoning. Make three diagonal slashes through the skin and flesh, on each side of the fish.

3 Preheat the broiler. Cut the butter into small pieces and insert into the slashes. Place fish in the broiler and cook under a high heat for 3–4 minutes on each side, depending on the thickness. Serve the fish with wedges of orange and new potatoes.

MACKEREL CALIFORNIA-STYLE

Fish well coated with spices are often fried until 'blackened' in California, but this does make a lot of smoke and smell in your kitchen. This recipe doesn't go quite that far!

──────── INGREDIENTS ────────

Serves 2–4

2 tsp paprika
1½ tsp salt
½ tsp each of onion powder,
   garlic powder, white pepper, black
   pepper, dried dill and dried oregano
2 large, thick mackerel, boned and
   filleted
½ cup butter
lemon slices and oregano, to garnish

1 Mix all the seasonings together. Dip each fillet of mackerel into the spice mixture until well coated.

2 Heat half of the butter in a large frying pan until really hot. Add the fish and cook two fillets at a time for about 2 minutes each side. Remove immediately, add the rest of the butter and then cook the other fillets.

3 Serve piping hot with a little of the butter from the pan poured over, and garnished with lemon slices and sprigs of oregano.

COOK'S TIP
Use a ready-prepared Cajun spice mix or sauce, if you prefer. Other fish like salmon, red snapper and tuna are also suitable, but thick cuts are best.

BAKED TROUT WITH OLIVES

INGREDIENTS

Serves 4

1 cup fresh whole wheat
*   breadcrumbs*
1oz chopped ham
½ cup finely chopped black olives
1 garlic clove, crushed
1 egg yolk
4 trout (about 6oz each)
½ cup dry vermouth
2 tbsp butter
1 tbsp flour
⅔ cup fish stock
3–4 tbsp light cream
salt and black pepper

1 Preheat the oven to 350°F. Mix the breadcrumbs, ham, olives, garlic, egg yolk and seasoning together. Pack into the trout cavities and place each one on a sheet of greased foil.

2 Pour 1 tbsp dry vermouth over each one, dot with half of the butter and wrap up closely. Bake for 20–25 minutes, or until tender.

3 Melt the remaining butter in a small pan and blend in the flour. Whisk in the remaining vermouth, the stock and the juices which have come out of the fish during cooking and cook for 1–2 minutes until thickened.

4 Stir in the cream, then season the sauce to taste and pour a little over each fish before serving hot.

SALMON CAKES WITH BUTTER SAUCE

Salmon fish cakes make a real treat for supper or a leisurely breakfast at the weekend. You could use any small tail pieces which are on sale.

INGREDIENTS

Makes 6

8oz tail piece of salmon, cooked
2 tbsp chopped fresh parsley
2 scallions, trimmed and chopped
grated rind and juice of ½ lemon
8oz mashed potato (not too soft)
1 egg, beaten
1 cup fresh white breadcrumbs
6 tbsp butter

1 Remove all the skin and bones from the fish and mash or flake it well. Add the parsley, scallions and 1 tsp of the lemon rind and season with salt and black pepper.

2 Gently work in the potato and then shape into six rounds, triangles or croquettes. Chill for 20 minutes.

3 Coat well in egg and then the breadcrumbs. Broil gently for 5 minutes each side, or until golden, or fry in butter and oil.

4 To make the butter sauce, melt the butter, whisk in the remaining lemon rind, the lemon juice, 1–2 tbsp water and seasoning to taste. Simmer for a few minutes and serve with the hot fish cakes.

PASTA, PIZZAS AND GRAINS

Simple ingredients from all over the world are now being advocated as the best forms of healthy nourishment. This collection includes classics like the Mushroom and Bacon Risotto and a selection of pizzas for quick home baking. There are very easy pasta dishes from a vegetarian lasagne to tortellini with a no-cook cheese sauce. Legumes and beans have come into their own recently and you don't need to be vegetarian to enjoy many, like Spiced Lentils with Sweet Onions, or Chick-peas and Artichokes au Gratin. So keep a good supply of dry beans and cereals, or their canned alternatives, and you will find that many of these dishes can be made at short notice from your well-stocked shelves, or can be easily increased to feed ten instead of four or six.

TUNA AND SHRIMP PIZZA

Serves 4
2 cups flour
1 tsp salt
½ package Rapid-Rise yeast
1 tbsp olive oil

For the topping
*5–6 tbsp ready-made tomato
  pizza sauce*
*7oz can tuna in water, partly
  drained*
4oz cooked, peeled shrimp
4 tbsp grated Cheddar cheese
4 tbsp diced mozzarella cheese
1 large garlic clove, crushed
1–2 tbsp olive oil
1 tbsp snipped fresh chives
1 tbsp chopped fresh parsley
salt and black pepper

1 To make the pizza dough, sift the flour into a bowl and stir in the salt and yeast. Then stir in the oil and up to ⅔ cup lukewarm water.

2 Gradually bring the dough together into a ball and knead for 5–10 minutes, until smooth and springy. Roll or stretch out to a 10in circle and place on a greased baking sheet.

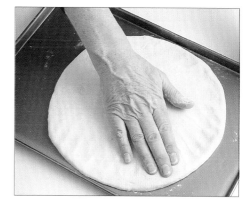

3 Preheat the oven to 425°F. Spread the tomato pizza sauce over the base, then the tuna. Arrange the shrimp on top and the two different cheeses.

4 Mix the garlic, oil, seasoning and herbs together and spoon all over the pizza. Leave the pizza to stand in a warm place for about 5 minutes, then cook for 15–20 minutes, until the base is crisp and the top melting.

COOK'S TIP
The basic pizza dough is suitable for all types of pizza and takes only minutes to mix together.

DEEP PAN VEGETABLE PIZZA

Serves 4

6oz pizza dough (see Cook's Tip)
½ cup canned creamed mushrooms
½ cup each cooked green beans,
* cauliflower florets, yellow pepper,*
* seeded and chopped, and baby*
* corn*
6–8 tiny tomatoes, halved
2–3 pieces sun-dried tomato in oil
2 tbsp ready-made tomato pizza
* sauce*
½ cup grated blue cheese
little oil
salt and black pepper

1 Stretch out the pizza dough and use to line an 7in deep pizza pan, or a shallow loose-based cake pan. Spread the pizza base with the creamed mushrooms.

2 Arrange the cooked vegetables neatly over the top and sprinkle with seasoning. Add the halved tomatoes and the sun-dried tomato cut into tiny pieces.

3 Drizzle the tomato sauce over the top and sprinkle on the cheese. Brush with oil where necessary and sprinkle with the seasoning. Leave in a warm place for the dough to rise up to the top of the pan.

4 Meanwhile, preheat the oven to 425°F. Bake the pizza for 15–20 minutes, until golden all over, bubbling in the middle and becoming quite crispy at the edges.

COOK'S TIP
To make a quick pizza dough, mix together 1½ cups flour, 1 tsp salt and half a package of Rapid-Rise yeast. Stir in 1 tbsp oil and up to ½ cup lukewarm water. Mix to a soft dough, then knead for about 5 minutes until smooth.

BAKED EGG PIZZA

INGREDIENTS

Serves 1
2oz pizza dough (see below)
olive oil
¼ cup sliced meat, such as bacon,
  mortadella, salami or pastrami
1 egg
2 tbsp mozzarella cheese, chopped
1 tsp chopped fresh parsley
salt and black pepper

COOK'S TIP
To make enough dough for three
pizzas, mix 1½ cups flour, 1 tsp salt
and ½ package of Rapid-Rise yeast.
Stir in 1 tbsp oil and up to ½ cup
lukewarm water. Mix to a soft
dough and knead until smooth.

1 Preheat the oven to 425°F. Roll or
stretch out the dough to a 6–7in
round. Place on a greased baking sheet.
Pinch up the edges, then brush the base
with oil.

2 Chop the meat over one half of the
dough. Have all the remaining
ingredients ready and crack the egg into
the centre. Be careful that the egg does
not run out while sprinkling with the
cheese, parsley and seasoning.

3 Fold over the dough, press the edges
to seal, then crimp. Brush with oil
and bake for 8–10 minutes, or until
golden and crisp. Serve at once.

SPICED LENTILS WITH SWEET ONIONS

INGREDIENTS

Serves 3–4
2 tbsp sunflower oil
1 small onion, chopped
2 garlic cloves, crushed
1 cup green lentils
2¼ cups good stock (beef, poultry or
  vegetable)
⅔ cup red wine
1 tsp chopped fresh sage, or a pinch of
  dried
8oz pearl onions, peeled
4 tbsp butter
4 tbsp light brown sugar
salt and black pepper
¼ cup salted cashew nuts and a few
  sprigs of thyme, to garnish

1 Heat the oil in a flameproof casserole and fry the onion and garlic
until softening. Add the lentils and fry
over a low heat for 3 minutes.

2 Stir in the stock, red wine, sage and
seasoning. Bring to a boil. Cover
and simmer gently for 20 minutes, stirring occasionally, until the lentils are
tender. Add more liquid if necessary.

3 Meanwhile, in a small frying pan
gently fry the pearl onions with the
butter and sugar for 5–7 minutes, until
the sugar begins to caramelise and the
onions are just tender. Stir occasionally.

4 Serve the lentils sprinkled with the
cashew nuts, garnished with thyme
sprigs, and accompanied by the onions.

Eggplant Lasagne

Serves 4

3 medium eggplants, sliced
5 tbsp olive oil
2 large onions, finely chopped
2 x 14oz cans chopped tomatoes
1 tsp dried mixed herbs
2–3 garlic cloves, crushed
6 sheets fresh lasagne
salt and black pepper

For the cheese sauce
2 tbsp butter
2 tbsp plain flour
1¼ cups milk
½ tsp made English mustard
8 tbsp grated sharp Cheddar cheese
1 tbsp grated Parmesan cheese

1 Layer the sliced eggplant in a colander, sprinkling lightly with salt between each layer. Leave to stand for 1 hour, then rinse and pat dry.

2 Heat 4 tbsp oil in a large pan, fry the eggplant and drain on kitchen paper. Add the remaining oil to the pan, cook the onions for 5 minutes, then stir in the tomatoes, herbs, garlic and seasoning. Bring to a boil and simmer, covered for 30 minutes.

3 Meanwhile, make the cheese sauce; melt the butter in a pan, stir in the flour and cook gently for 1 minute, stirring. Gradually stir in the milk. Bring to a boil, stirring, and cook for 2 minutes. Remove from the heat and stir in the mustard, cheeses and seasoning.

4 Preheat the oven to 400°F. Arrange half the eggplants in the base of an ovenproof dish, spoon over half the tomato sauce. Arrange three sheets of lasagne on top. Repeat with a second layer.

5 Spoon over the cheese sauce, cover and bake for 30 minutes. Remove the lid for the last 10 minutes to brown the crust. Serve hot with a mixed salad.

> **Freezer Note**
> This dish freezes well; cook for only 20 minutes, cool, then freeze. Reheat at 375°F for 20 minutes; increase the temperature to 400°F for 10 minutes to brown the top.

NOODLES WITH SHRIMP IN LEMON SAUCE

As in many Chinese dishes the fish is here purely for color and a little flavor. You could serve this as an accompaniment with several others, or as part of a Chinese-style menu.

INGREDIENTS

Serves 4

2 packages Chinese egg noodles
1 tbsp sunflower oil
2 stalks celery, cut into matchsticks
2 garlic cloves, crushed
4 scallions, sliced
2 carrots, cut into matchsticks
3in piece cucumber, cut into
   matchsticks
4oz shrimp in shells
1 lemon, or 2 tbsp lemon sauce
1 tsp cornstarch
4–5 tbsp fish stock
1 cup shelled shrimp
salt and black pepper
few sprigs dill, to garnish

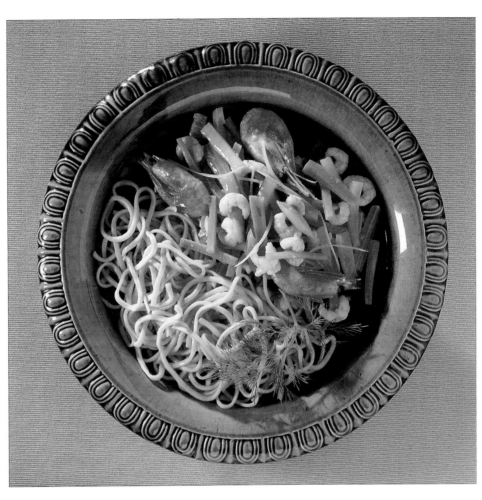

1 Put the noodles in boiling water and leave to soak as directed on the package. Meanwhile, heat the oil in a pan and stir-fry the celery, garlic, scallions and carrots for 2–3 minutes.

2 Add the cucumber and whole shrimp and cook for 2–3 minutes. Meanwhile, peel the rind from the lemon and cut into long thin shreds. Place in boiling water for 1 minute.

3 Blend the lemon juice, or lemon sauce, with the cornstarch and stock and add to the pan. Bring gently to a boil, stirring, and cook for 1 minute.

4 Stir in the shelled shrimp, the drained lemon rind and seasoning to taste. Drain the noodles and serve with the shrimp, garnished with dill.

COOK'S TIP
These noodles can also be deep-fried. Once cooked as above, drain on kitchen paper. Deep-fry small amounts at a time, until golden brown and very crisp.

PASTA WITH DEVILED KIDNEYS

INGREDIENTS

Serves 4

8–10 lamb's kidneys
1 tbsp sunflower oil
2 tbsp butter
2 tsp paprika
1–2 tsp mild grainy mustard
salt
8oz fresh pasta, to serve
chopped fresh parsley, to garnish

1 Cut the kidneys in half and neatly cut out the white cores with scissors. Cut the kidneys again if very large.

2 Heat the oil and butter together. Add the kidneys and cook, turning frequently, for about 2 minutes. Blend the paprika and mustard together with a little salt and stir into the pan.

3 Continue cooking the kidneys, basting frequently, for 3–4 minutes.

4 Cook the pasta for 10–12 minutes, or according to the instructions on the package. Serve the kidneys and their sauce, topped with the chopped parsley, and accompanied by the pasta.

GOLDEN-TOPPED PASTA

When it comes to the children helping plan the menus, this is the sort of dish that wins hands down. It is also perfect for 'padding out' if you have to feed eight instead of four.

INGREDIENTS

Serves 4–6

8oz dried pasta shells or spirals
4oz chopped ham, beef or turkey
3 cups par-boiled mixed vegetables, such as carrots, cauliflower, beans, corn etc
little oil

For the cheese sauce
2 tbsp butter
2 tbsp flour
1¼ cups milk
1½ cups grated Cheddar cheese
1–2 tsp mustard
salt and black pepper

1 Cook the pasta according to the instructions on the package. Drain well and place in a large flameproof dish with the chopped ham, vegetables and 1-2 tsp oil.

2 To make the cheese sauce, melt the butter in a saucepan, stir in the flour and cook gently for 1 minute, stirring. Remove the pan from the heat and gradually stir in the milk, bring to a boil, stirring, and cook for 2 minutes. Add half the grated cheese, the mustard and seasoning to taste.

3 Spoon the sauce over the meat and vegetables. Sprinkle with the rest of the cheese and broil quickly until golden and bubbling.

MUSHROOM AND BACON RISOTTO

INGREDIENTS

Serves 4

2 tbsp sunflower oil
1 large onion, chopped
3oz smoked bacon, chopped
12oz Arborio or risotto rice
1–2 garlic cloves, crushed
¼ cup dried sliced mushrooms, soaked
   in a little boiling water
6oz mixed fresh mushrooms
5 cups hot stock
few sprigs of oregano or thyme
1 tbsp butter
little dry white wine
3 tbsp chopped, peeled tomato
8–10 black olives, pitted and quartered
salt and black pepper
sprigs of thyme, to garnish

1 Heat the oil in a large, heavy-based pan with a lid. Gently cook the onion and bacon until the onion is tender and the bacon fat has run out.

2 Stir in the rice and garlic and cook over a high heat for 2–3 minutes, until the rice is well coated. Add the dried mushrooms and their liquid, the fresh mushrooms and half the stock, the oregano and seasoning. Bring gently to a boil, then reduce the heat to minimum. Cover tightly and leave to cook.

3 Check the liquid in the risotto occasionally by very gently stirring. If quite dry, slowly add more liquid. (Don't stir too often, as this lets the steam and flavor out.) Add more liquid as required until the rice is cooked, but not mushy.

4 Just before serving, stir in the butter, white wine, tomatoes and olives and check the seasoning. Serve hot, garnished with thyme sprigs.

GOLDEN VEGETABLE PAELLA

INGREDIENTS

Serves 4

*pinch of saffron strands or 1 tsp ground
    turmeric*
3⅔ cups hot vegetable or spicy stock
6 tbsp olive oil
2 large onions, sliced
3 garlic cloves, chopped
1⅓ cups long grain rice
⅓ cup wild rice
*6oz pumpkin or butternut squash,
    chopped*
6oz carrots, cut in matchsticks
1 yellow bell pepper, seeded and sliced
4 tomatoes, peeled and chopped
4oz oyster mushrooms, quartered
salt and black pepper
*strips of red, yellow and green bell
    pepper, to garnish*

1 Place the saffron in a small bowl with 3–4 tbsp boiling hot stock. Leave to stand for 5 minutes. Meanwhile, heat the oil in a paella pan or large heavy-based frying pan. Fry the onions and garlic gently until just softening.

2 Add the rices and toss for 2–3 minutes until coated in oil. Add the stock to the pan with the pumpkin or squash, and the saffron strands and liquid. Stir as it comes to a boil and reduce the heat to the minimum.

3 Cover with a pan lid or foil and cook very gently for about 15 minutes. (Avoid stirring unnecessarily as this lets out the steam and moistness.) Add the carrots, bell pepper, tomatoes, salt and black pepper, cover again and leave for a further 5 minutes, or until the rice is almost tender.

4 Finally, add the oyster mushrooms, check the seasoning and cook, uncovered, for just enough time to soften the mushrooms without letting the paella stick. Top with the peppers and serve as soon as possible.

Spaghetti with Tomato Sauce

Don't be put off by the idea of anchovies, they give a wonderful richness to the sauce, without adding their usual salty flavor.

Ingredients

Serves 4
3 tbsp olive oil
1 onion, chopped
1 large garlic clove, chopped
14oz can chopped tomatoes with herbs
4 tbsp dry white wine
12oz dried spaghetti
1–2 tsp dark brown sugar
2oz can anchovy fillets in oil
4oz peperoni sausage, chopped
1 tbsp chopped fresh basil
salt and black pepper
sprigs of basil, to garnish

1 Heat the oil in a saucepan and fry the onion and garlic for 2 minutes to soften. Add the tomatoes and wine, bring to a boil and leave to simmer gently for 10–15 minutes. Put the pasta on to cook as directed.

2 After the sauce has been cooking for 10 minutes, add the brown sugar and the anchovy fillets, drained and chopped. Mix well and cook for a further 5 minutes or so.

3 Drain the pasta and toss in very little oil. Add to it the peperoni and the basil and sprinkle with seasoning. Serve topped with the tomato sauce and garnish with the sprigs of basil.

Tortellini with Cheese Sauce

Here is a very quick way of making a delicious cheese sauce without all the usual effort. But do eat it when really hot before the sauce starts to thicken up. Blue cheese would work well, too.

Ingredients

Serves 4
1 lb fresh tortellini
4oz ricotta or cream cheese
4–6 tbsp milk
½ cup St Paulin or mozzarella cheese, grated
½ cup Parmesan cheese, grated
2 garlic cloves, crushed
2 tbsp chopped, mixed fresh herbs, such as parsley, chives, basil or oregano
salt and black pepper

1 Cook the pasta according to the package instructions, in boiling, salted water, stirring occasionally.

2 Meanwhile, gently melt the ricotta or cream cheese with the milk in a large pan. When blended, stir in the St Paulin or mozzarella, half the Parmesan, and the garlic and herbs.

3 Drain the cooked pasta and add to the pan of sauce. Stir well, allowing one or two minutes of gentle cooking for the cheeses to melt well. Season to taste and serve with the rest of the Parmesan cheese sprinkled on top.

Bacon and Egg Bread Pudding

Bacon and egg is such an obvious combination, but perhaps not often thought of as a bread pudding. But it is delicious and could use up leftover ingredients.

—— Ingredients ——

Serves 4
8 rashers bacon, crisply grilled, rinded and chopped
5–6 slices bread, buttered
2 eggs
1¼ cups milk
1 garlic clove, crushed
½ cup grated Cheddar cheese
salt and black pepper

1 Sandwich the bacon between the bread slices, cut into triangles and arrange in a buttered ovenproof dish.

2 Mix the eggs, milk and garlic, and season to taste. Pour this mixture over the bread and leave to soak up for about 10 minutes. Meanwhile, preheat the oven to 350°F.

3 Sprinkle the grated cheese over the top of the bread pudding and bake for 30–40 minutes, until golden brown. (Finish off under the broiler if it needs further browning.)

Chick-Peas and Artichokes au Gratin

For last-minute extras this is a very quick, extremely tasty, and unusual dish.

—— Ingredients ——

Serves 4
14oz can chick-peas, drained
14oz can black-eyed peas, drained
4½oz jar marinated artichokes (or canned artichoke hearts, chopped, plus a little olive oil)
1 red bell spepper, seeded and chopped
1 garlic clove, crushed
1 tbsp chopped fresh parsley
1 tsp lemon juice
⅔ cup sour cream
1 egg yolk
½ cup grated cheese
salt and black pepper

1 Preheat the oven to 350°F. Mix the chick-peas, black-eyed peas, marinated artichokes or artichoke hearts, and bell pepper together.

2 Stir in as much of the artichoke dressing, or oil if using artichoke hearts, as is necessary to moisten the mixture. Stir in the garlic, parsley, lemon juice and seasoning to taste.

3 Mix together the sour cream, egg yolk, cheese and seasoning. Spoon evenly over the vegetables and bake for 25–30 minutes, or until the top is golden brown.

VEGETABLES AND SALADS

Vegetables are so wonderfully colorful that it is fun to cook with them. However, children and teenagers never seem to have quite the same sort of enthusiasm for vegetables, so we have to try and tempt them with familiar-looking yet delicious-tasting ideas. Garlic Baked Tomatoes, or Leek and Stilton Triangles, Lemon Carrot Salad, or ratatouille cooked so quickly it is more of a salad, may be good tempters to start with. We are lucky to have a vast selection of vegetables and a huge collection of salads all year round to choose from. Encourage your family to try new varieties by buying a new 'leaf' or 'green' occasionally. Let them choose and make their own salad or vegetable selection for supper – then they can't leave any on the plate!

APPLE, ONION AND GRUYÈRE TART

Serves 4–6
2 cups flour
¼ tsp dry mustard
6 tbsp soft margarine
6 tbsp Gruyère cheese, finely grated

For the filling
2 tbsp butter
1 large onion, finely chopped
1 large or 2 small eating apples, peeled
   and grated
2 eggs
⅔ cup heavy cream
¼ tsp dried mixed herbs
½ tsp dry mustard
4oz Gruyère cheese
salt and black pepper

1 To make the pastry, sift the flour, salt and dry mustard into a bowl. Rub in the margarine and cheese until the mixture forms soft breadcrumbs. Add 2 tbsp water and bring together into a ball. Chill, covered or wrapped, for 30 minutes.

2 Meanwhile, make the filling; melt the butter in a pan, add the onion and cook gently for 10 minutes, stirring occasionally, until softened but not browned. Stir in the apple and cook for 2–3 minutes. Leave to cool.

3 Roll out the pastry and use to line a lightly greased 8in fluted quiche pan. Chill for 20 minutes. Preheat the oven to 400°F.

4 Line the pastry with wax paper and fill with baking beans. Bake the pie shell for 20 minutes.

5 Beat together the eggs, cream, herbs, seasoning and mustard. Grate three-quarters of the cheese and stir into the egg mixture, then slice the remaining cheese and set aside. When the pastry is cooked, remove the paper and beans and pour in the egg mixture.

6 Arrange the sliced cheese over the top. Reduce the oven temperature to 375°F. Return the tart to the oven and cook for a further 20 minutes, until the filling is golden and just firm. Serve hot or warm.

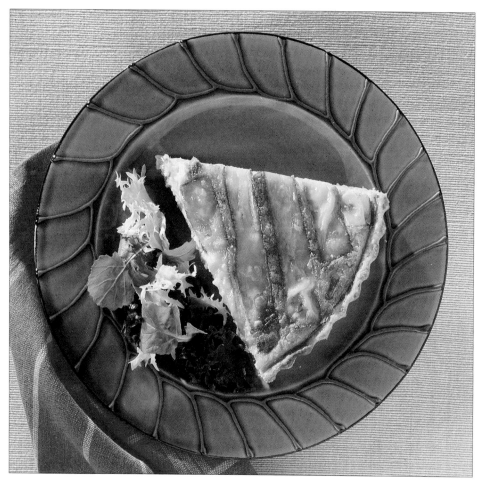

> COOK'S TIP
> You could substitute other hard cheeses, such as Cheddar, Provolone, or Emmenthaler for the Gruyère, if you prefer.

LEEK AND STILTON TRIANGLES

These tasty triangles make great party nibbles, especially if you prepare them well in advance and freeze them ready to cook. Use another type of cheese if your family doesn't like Stilton.

INGREDIENTS

Makes 16
2 leeks, sliced
2 tbsp milk
1 tbsp orange juice
¾ cup Stilton cheese, crumbled or diced
8 sheets filo pastry
2 tbsp butter, melted
black pepper

1 Very gently cook the leeks in the milk and orange juice for about 8–10 minutes until really soft, then season with pepper. Allow to cool slightly before mixing in the Stilton.

2 Lay out one sheet of pastry flat, brush it with butter and cut in half to make a long oblong strip. Place one-sixteenth of the leek and Stilton mixture in the bottom right hand corner. Fold the corner point up and over the filling towards the left edge to form a triangular shape.

3 Next, fold the bottom left hand point up to give a straight bottom edge to the pastry sheet, then fold the pastry triangle over to the right and then up again, so that the filling is completely enclosed.

4 Preheat the oven to 400°F. Continue folding up the sheet of pastry and tuck the top flap underneath. Brush with very little butter and place on a baking sheet.

5 Repeat this process for the rest of the pastry and filling mixture, to make about 16 triangles in all.

6 Bake the triangles for 10–15 minutes, until golden brown and crisp. Serve hot as a starter, or to pass round with drinks.

FREEZER NOTE
To freeze, stack the uncooked triangles between sheets of wax paper and then wrap tightly in plastic wrap. Freeze for up to 6 months. Defrost for 1 hour before cooking for 12–18 minutes, until hot and golden brown.

CHEESE POTATO SLICES

Potato slices are ideal for a quick kids' snack, or a main meal accompaniment.

INGREDIENTS

Serves 4
2 large potatoes, baked until almost cooked, then cooled
2 tbsp sunflower oil
1 garlic clove, crushed
6 tbsp grated sharp Cheddar cheese
salt and black pepper

1 Preheat the oven to 375°F. Slice the potatoes lengthwise about ½in thick and brush one side with oil. Arrange on baking sheets.

2 Mix the rest of the oil with the garlic and seasoning. Brush over the tops of the potatoes.

3 Sprinkle the cheese evenly over the potatoes and bake for about 15–20 minutes, or until the cheese topping is golden and bubbling.

COOK'S TIP
If you prefer, these potato slices can be cooked under a hot broiler, or on a barbecue for 7–10 minutes.

ZUCCHINI AND PEPPERS AU GRATIN

INGREDIENTS

Serves 4
4 small zucchini, sliced
1 red pepper, seeded and sliced
1 green pepper, seeded and sliced
1 tbsp olive oil
1 tsp walnut or hazelnut oil
5 tbsp sour cream
1–2 tbsp milk
1 tsp grated lime rind
2 tbsp flaked almonds
salt and black pepper

1 Mix the zucchini and peppers together. Add the oils and seasoning and toss well until the vegetables are thoroughly coated in oil.

2 Preheat the oven to 350°F. Blend the cream and a little milk together to give a pouring consistency. Add the lime rind and seasoning and pour evenly over the vegetables.

3 Sprinkle with the almonds and bake for 30 minutes, until the top is golden and the vegetables tender.

COOK'S TIP
To make this dish into a more substantial meal, top with a layer of sliced, cooked potatoes and a cheese sauce, in place of the sour cream and lime.

BAKED ZUCCHINI

Creamy baked zucchini are lovely for a starter or the perfect accompaniment to simple fish and grilled meat dishes.

INGREDIENTS

Serves 4
3 tbsp butter
1 leek, finely chopped
2 large or 4 medium zucchini, trimmed and coarsely grated
2 tbsp flour
⅔ cup milk
1 tsp English mustard
1 tbsp ricotta
2 tsp chopped fresh basil
1 tsp caraway seeds (optional)
3 eggs, separated
salt and black pepper

1 Melt the butter in a medium to large pan, add the leek and cook for 2 minutes, stirring. Add the zucchini and flour and cook for a further 2 minutes, stirring.

2 Gradually stir in the milk, then bring to a boil, stirring to make sure there are no lumps, and cook for 2 minutes. Remove from the heat.

3 Season with salt, pepper and mustard, stir in the ricotta, basil and caraway seeds, if using. Beat in the egg yolks. Preheat the oven to 375°F.

4 Whisk the egg whites until they form stiff peaks. Using a metal spoon, carefully fold the egg whites into the zucchini mixture.

5 Spoon into a 3 pint casserole or ovenproof dish. Bake for 30–35 minutes, until well risen and golden brown. Serve immediately.

CRACKED WHEAT WITH FENNEL

INGREDIENTS

Serves 4

¾ cup cracked wheat
1 large fennel bulb, finely chopped
4oz green beans, chopped and blanched
1 small orange
1 garlic clove, crushed
2–3 tbsp sunflower oil
1 tbsp white wine vinegar
salt and black pepper
½ red or orange pepper, seeded and
   finely chopped, to garnish

1 Place the wheat in a bowl and cover with boiling water. Leave for 10–15 minutes, stirring occasionally. When doubled in size, drain well and squeeze out any excess water.

2 While still slightly warm, stir in the chopped fennel and the green beans. Finely grate the orange rind into a bowl. Peel and segment the orange and stir into the salad.

3 Add the crushed garlic to the orange rind, then add the sunflower oil, white wine vinegar, and seasoning to taste, and mix thoroughly. Pour this dressing over the salad, mix well. Chill the salad for 1–2 hours.

4 Serve the salad sprinkled with the chopped red or orange pepper.

NEW POTATO PARCELS

Even with the oven packed full, you should still be able to find a corner for these delicious potatoes. If necessary, cook them in individual portions. They could be put over a barbecue or real fire, too, and left for long slow cooking.

INGREDIENTS

Serves 4

16–20 very small potatoes in their skins
4 tbsp olive oil
1–2 sprigs each of thyme, tarragon and oregano, or 1 tbsp mixed dried herbs
salt and black pepper

1 Preheat the oven to 400°F. Grease one large sheet or four small sheets of foil.

2 Put the potatoes in a large bowl and add the rest of the ingredients and seasonings. Mix well so the potatoes are thoroughly coated.

3 Put the potatoes into the middle of the foil and seal up the parcel(s). Place on a baking sheet and bake for 40–50 minutes. The potatoes will stay warm in the parcel for quite some time.

STIR-FRIED FLORETS WITH HAZELNUTS

A rich hazelnut dressing turns crunchy cauliflower and broccoli into a very special vegetable dish.

INGREDIENTS

Serves 4

1½ cups cauliflower florets
1½ cups broccoli florets
1 tbsp sunflower oil
½ cup hazelnuts, finely chopped
¼ red chili, finely chopped, or 1 tsp chili powder (optional)
4 tbsp crème fraîche or sour cream
salt and black pepper
thin rings of chili or chopped red pepper, to garnish

1 Make sure the cauliflower and broccoli florets are all of an even size. Heat the oil in a saucepan or wok and toss the florets over a high heat for 1 minute.

2 Reduce the heat and continue stir-frying for another 5 minutes, then add the hazelnuts, chili and seasoning.

3 When the cauliflower is crisp and nearly tender, stir in the crème fraîche or sour cream and just heat through. Serve at once, sprinkled with the chili rings or chopped pepper.

COOK'S TIP
The crisper these florets are the better, so cook them just long enough to make them piping hot, and give them time to absorb all the flavors.

WARM CHICKEN LIVER SALAD

Although warm salads may seem over-fussy or trendy, there are times when they are just right. Serve this delicious combination as either a starter or a light meal, with hunks of bread to dip into the dressing.

INGREDIENTS

Serves 4

4oz each fresh young spinach leaves, arugula and red leaf lettuce
2 pink grapefruit
6 tbsp sunflower oil
2 tsp sesame oil
2 tsp soy sauce
8oz chicken livers, chopped
salt and black pepper

1 Wash, dry and tear up all the leaves. Mix them together well in a large salad bowl.

2 Carefully cut away all the peel and white pith from the grapefruit, then neatly segment them catching all the juices in a bowl. Add the grapefruit segments to the leaves in the bowl.

3 To make the dressing, mix together 4 tbsp of the sunflower oil with the sesame oil, soy sauce, seasoning and grapefruit juice to taste.

4 Heat the rest of the sunflower oil in a small pan and cook the liver, stirring gently, until firm and lightly browned.

5 Tip the chicken livers and dressing over the salad and serve at once.

> ### COOK'S TIP
> Chicken or turkey livers are often sold frozen. They are ideal for this recipe, and there's no need to leave them to defrost completely before cooking.

GREEN GREEN SALAD

You could make this lovely dish at any time of the year using imported or frozen vegetables and still get a pretty, healthy – and unusual – salad.

INGREDIENTS

Serves 4

6oz shelled fava beans
4oz green beans, quartered
4oz snow peas
8–10 small fresh mint leaves
3 scallions, chopped
4 tbsp green olive oil
1 tbsp cider vinegar
1 tbsp chopped fresh mint, or 1 tsp dried
1 garlic clove, crushed
salt and black pepper

1 Plunge the fava beans into a saucepan of boiling water and bring back to the boil. Remove from the heat immediately and plunge the beans into cold water. Drain. Repeat with the green beans.

COOK'S TIP
Frozen fava beans are a good stand-by, but for this salad try to find time to pop them out of their outer shells.

2 Mix together the blanched beans, the raw snow peas, mint leaves and scallions.

3 Mix together the olive oil, vinegar, chopped mint, garlic and seasoning thoroughly, then pour over the salad and toss well. Chill until ready to serve.

QUICK RATATOUILLE SALAD

Similar but different, quick but delicious is this salad. The key thing is that it keeps well; in fact, it improves if eaten the next day.

INGREDIENTS

Serves 4

1 small eggplant, about 8oz
salt
4 tbsp olive oil
1 onion, sliced
1 green bell pepper, seeded and cut in strips
3 garlic cloves, crushed
1–2 tbsp cider vinegar
8 tiny firm tomatoes, halved
salt and mixed ground peppercorns
sprigs of oregano, to garnish

1 Slice and quarter the eggplant. Place in a colander and sprinkle with plenty of salt. Leave for 20 minutes and then drain off any liquid and rinse well under cold water.

2 Heat the oil in a large pan and gently sauté the onion, pepper and garlic, then stir in the eggplant and toss over a high heat for 5 minutes.

3 When the eggplant is beginning to turn golden, add the cider vinegar, tomatoes and seasoning to taste. Leave to cool, then chill well. Season to taste again before serving, garnished with sprigs of oregano.

> **COOK'S TIP**
> Once the eggplants are rinsed, squeeze them dry between sheets of paper towel – the drier they are, the quicker they will cook and brown.

CRISP FRUITY SALAD

Crisp lettuce, tangy cheese and crunchy pieces of fruit make a refreshing anytime salad.

INGREDIENTS

Serves 4

½ Bibb lettuce
3oz grapes, seeded and halved
½ cup sharp Cheddar cheese, grated
1 large eating apple, cored and thinly sliced
6–7 tbsp mild French vinaigrette (see Cook's Tip)
3 tbsp garlic croûtons

1 Tear the lettuce leaves into small pieces and place in a salad bowl. Add the grapes, cheese and apples.

2 Pour the dressing over the salad. Mix well and serve at once, sprinkled with garlic croûtons.

> **COOK'S TIP**
> To make a light vinaigrette, mix 1 tbsp Dijon mustard, 1 tbsp white wine vinegar, a pinch of sugar, and seasoning with 4 tbsp sunflower oil.

GARLIC BAKED TOMATOES

If you can find them, use Italian plum tomatoes, which have a warm, slightly sweet flavour. For large numbers of people you could use cherry tomatoes, not halved but tossed several times during cooking.

─ INGREDIENTS ─

Serves 4

3 tbsp sweet butter
1 large garlic clove, crushed
1 tsp finely grated orange rind
*4 firm plum tomatoes, or 2 large beef-
    steak tomatoes*
salt and black pepper
shredded basil leaves, to garnish

1 Soften the butter and blend with the crushed garlic, orange rind, and seasoning. Chill for a few minutes.

2 Preheat the oven to 400°F. Halve the tomatoes crosswise and trim the bases so they stand.

3 Place the tomatoes in an ovenproof dish and spread the butter equally over each tomato half.

4 Bake the tomatoes in the oven for 15–25 minutes, depending on the size of the tomato halves, until just tender. Serve sprinkled with the basil.

FREEZER NOTE
Garlic butter is well worth keeping in the freezer. Make it up as above, or omit the orange rind and add chopped fresh parsley. Freeze in thick slices or chunks ready to use, or roll into a sausage shape and wrap in foil, then cut into slices when partly defrosted.

LEMON CARROT SALAD

You don't need to be on a diet to enjoy this tangy, colorful and refreshing salad.

─ INGREDIENTS ─

Serves 4–6

1 lb baby carrots
grated rind and juice of ½ lemon
1 tbsp light brown sugar
4 tbsp sunflower oil
1 tsp hazelnut or sesame oil
*1 tsp chopped fresh oregano,
    or pinch of dried*
salt and black pepper

1 Finely grate the carrots and place them in a large bowl. Stir in the lemon rind, 1–2 tbsp of the lemon juice, the sugar, sunflower and hazelnut or sesame oils, and mix well.

2 Add more lemon juice and seasoning to taste, then sprinkle on the oregano, toss lightly and leave the salad for 1 hour before serving.

COOK'S TIP
Other root vegetables could be used in this salad. For instance, you could try replacing half the carrot with rutabaga, or use celeriac, or kohlrabi instead.

HOT DESSERTS

Home-made desserts are often a rare treat nowadays, since we seldom have the time mid-week to cook and prepare two- or three-course meals. However, if your family pines for sweets, then you will find lots of inspiration here – on the following pages are some really fabulous, old-fashioned treats, such as Treacle and Oatmeal Tart, and Caramel Rice Pudding. There are also a few innovative, unusual combinations such as Apricot and Pear Filo Roulade, Hot Chocolate Cake with a white chocolate sauce, and Lemon and Orange Whole Wheat Tart. There are also a few lighter desserts for the calorie counters, who might like to try delicious Grilled Oranges with – or without! – Spiced Cream, and Warm Pears in Cider.

CHERRIES UNDER A SHORTBREAD CRUST

──── INGREDIENTS ────

Serves 8

1lb black or red cherries, pitted
¾ cup grape, apple or cranberry juice
3 tbsp cornstarch
grated rind of 1 orange
few drops of vanilla extract
1–2 tbsp sugar
2 cups flour, sifted
pinch of salt
¼ cup confectioner's sugar, sifted
1 scant cup butter
*4–6 tbsp heavy cream or crème fraîche,
    to serve*

1 Put the cherries in a 9in pie plate, piled high. Blend the fruit juice with 1 tbsp of the cornstarch, the orange rind and vanilla extract. Bring to a boil, stirring, until thickened. Sweeten with a little of the sugar. Leave to cool, then pour over the cherries.

2 Sift the remaining flours with the salt and confectioner's sugar, then gently rub in the butter and, when well distributed, bring together in a ball. Or process in a food processor for a few minutes until it comes together. Knead lightly, then wrap in plastic wrap and chill for 20 minutes.

3 Roll out the crust on a lightly floured surface, or between sheets of wax paper, to the size of the top of the pie plate.

4 Preheat the oven to 350°F. Brush the edge of the plate with water and carefully lay the pastry on top. Gently trim off the excess and then pinch up the edges well, pressing the pastry firmly on to the rim. Flute the edge, then mark the top into eight sections and make a hole in the centre.

5 Bake the pie for 20 minutes, then reduce the heat to 325°F for a further 20 minutes, until the top is golden and crisp. Sprinkle the top with sugar and serve hot with the cream or crème fraîche.

HOT CHOCOLATE CAKE

This is wonderfully wicked, either hot served with a white chocolate sauce, or cold. The basic cake freezes well – thaw, then warm in the microwave before serving.

INGREDIENTS

Makes 10–12 slices
1¼ cups self-rising whole wheat flour
¼ cup cocoa powder
pinch of salt
¼ cup soft margarine
¼ cup light brown sugar
few drops vanilla extract
4 eggs
3oz white chocolate, coarsely chopped
chocolate leaves and curls, to decorate

For the white chocolate sauce
3oz white chocolate
⅔ cup light cream
2–3 tbsp milk

1 Preheat the oven to 325°F. Sift the flour, cocoa powder and salt into a bowl, adding back in the whole wheat flakes from the sieve.

2 Cream the margarine, sugar and vanilla extract together until light and fluffy, then gently beat in one egg.

3 Gradually stir in the remaining eggs, one at a time, alternately folding in some of the flour, until all the flour mixture is well blended in.

4 Stir in the white chocolate and spoon into a 1½–2lb loaf pan or a 7in greased cake pan. Bake for 30–40 minutes, or until just firm to the touch and shrinking away from the sides of the pan.

5 Meanwhile, prepare the sauce; heat the chocolate and cream very gently in a pan until the chocolate is melted. Add the milk and stir until cool.

6 Serve the cake sliced, in a pool of sauce and decorated with chocolate leaves and curls.

PINEAPPLE FLAMBÉ

Flambéing means adding alcohol and then burning it off so the flavor is not too overpowering. This recipe is just as good, however, without the brandy – perfect if you wish to serve it to young children.

INGREDIENTS

Serves 4
1 large, ripe pineapple
3 tbsp sweet butter
3 tbsp brown sugar
4 tbsp fresh orange juice
2 tbsp brandy or vodka
2 tbsp slivered almonds, toasted

1 Cut away the top and base of the pineapple. Then cut down the sides, removing all the dark 'eyes', but leaving the pineapple in a good shape.

2 Cut the pineapple into thin slices and, with an apple corer, remove the hard central core.

3 In a large frying pan melt the butter, sugar and orange juice. Add the pineapple slices and cook for 1–2 minutes, turning once.

4 Add the brandy and light with a match immediately. Let the flames die down and then sprinkle with the almonds and serve with ice cream or thick yogurt.

WARM PEARS IN CIDER

INGREDIENTS

Serves 4
1 lemon
¼ cup sugar
grated nutmeg
1 cup sweet cider
4 firm, ripe pears
light cream, to serve

1 Carefully remove the rind from the lemon with a potato peeler leaving any white pith behind.

2 Squeeze the juice from the lemon into a saucepan, add the rind, sugar, nutmeg and cider and heat through to dissolve the sugar.

3 Carefully peel the pears, leaving the stalks on if possible, and place them in the pan of cider. Poach the pears for 10–15 minutes until almost tender, turning them frequently.

4 Transfer the pears to individual serving dishes using a slotted spoon. Simmer the liquid over a high heat until it reduces slightly and becomes syrupy.

5 Pour the warm syrup over the pears, and serve at once with freshly made custard, cream or ice cream.

COOK'S TIP
To get pears of just the right firmness, you may have to buy them slightly under-ripe and then wait a day or more. Soft pears are no good at all for this dish.

BLUEBERRY PANCAKES

These are rather like thick break-fast pancakes – though they can, of course, be eaten at any time of the day.

INGREDIENTS

Makes 6–8
1 cup self-rising flour
pinch of salt
3–4 tbsp sugar
2 eggs
½ cup milk
1–2 tbsp oil
4oz fresh or frozen blueberries
maple syrup, to serve

1 Sift the flour into a bowl with the salt and sugar. Beat together the eggs thoroughly. Make a well in the middle of the flour and stir in the eggs.

2 Gradually blend in a little of the milk to make a smooth batter. Then whisk in the rest of the milk and whisk for 1–2 minutes. Allow to rest for 20–30 minutes.

3 Heat a few drops of oil in a pancake pan or heavy-based frying pan until just hazy. Pour on about 2 tbsp of the batter and swirl the batter around until it makes an even shape.

4 Cook for 2–3 minutes and when almost set on top, sprinkle over 1–2 tbsp blueberries. As soon as the base is loose and golden brown, turn the pan-cake over.

5 Cook on the second side for only about 1 minute, until golden and crisp. Slide the pancake on to a plate and serve drizzled with maple syrup. Continue with the rest of the batter.

> COOK'S TIP
> Instead of blueberries you could use fresh or frozen blackberries or raspberries. If you use canned fruit, make sure it is very well drained or the liquid will run and color the pancakes.

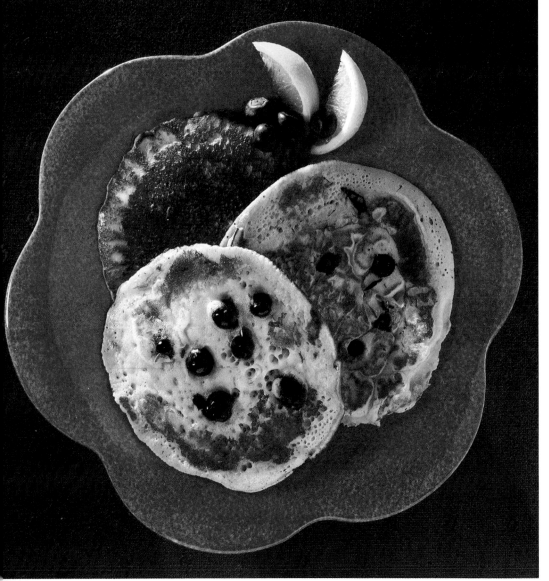

LEMON AND ORANGE WHOLE WHEAT TART

INGREDIENTS

Serves 8–10
1 cup flour, sifted
1 cup whole wheat flour
2 tbsp ground hazelnuts
3 tbsp confectioner's sugar, sifted
pinch of salt
½ cup sweet butter
4 tbsp lemon curd
1¼ cups whipped cream or ricotta
4 oranges, peeled and thinly sliced

1 Place the flours, hazelnuts, sugar, salt and butter in a food processor and process in short bursts until the mixture resembles breadcrumbs. Add 2–3 tbsp cold water and process until the dough comes together.

2 Turn out on to a lightly floured surface and knead gently until smooth. Roll out and line a 10in pie pan. Be sure not to stretch the pastry and gently ease it into the corners of the pie pan. Chill for 20 minutes. Preheat the oven to 375°F.

3 Line the pastry with wax paper and fill with baking beans or bread crusts. Bake for 15 minutes, remove the paper and continue for a further 5–10 minutes, until the pastry is crisp. Allow to cool.

4 Whisk the lemon curd into the cream or ricotta and spread over the base of the pastry. Arrange the orange slices on top and serve at room temperature.

Grilled Oranges with Spiced Cream

Ingredients

Serves 4

3 large oranges
1–2 tbsp raw sugar
⅔ cup thick or sour cream, crème
  fraîche or Greek-style yogurt
1 tsp mixed spice
few drops vanilla extract
sugar, to taste

1 Cut away all the orange rind and white pith using a sharp knife, saving any of the juices. Cut the oranges into thick slices and arrange these on foil in a broiler pan.

2 Sprinkle the orange slices with the sugar. Whisk the cream, crème fraîche or yogurt until smooth, then blend in the mixed spice and vanilla extract and any orange juice. Chill.

3 Place the orange slices under a very hot broiler and broil until browned and bubbling. Transfer the orange slices to serving plates and serve at once with the chilled spiced cream.

Treacle and Oatmeal Tart

Oatmeal always evokes childhood memories. This tart, with its rich molasses flavor, is a far cry from the dutiful hot cereal served on cold winter mornings.

Ingredients

Serves 6–8

1 cup flour
⅔ cup rolled oats
pinch of salt
½ cup butter or margarine
6 tbsp corn syrup
2 tbsp black molasses
grated rind and juice of 1 orange
1½ cups soft white bread or cake
  crumbs

1 Place the flour, oats, salt and fat in a food processor and process on high for ½–1 minute, until well blended.

2 Turn into a bowl and stir in sufficient water (4–5 tbsp) to bring the pastry together. Knead lightly until smooth, wrap in plastic wrap and chill for 10–20 minutes.

3 Place the syrup, molasses, orange rind and juice in a pan and warm through. Then stir in the crumbs. Preheat the oven to 375°F.

4 Roll out the pastry on a floured surface to a 9in round and use to line a shallow 8in pie plate. Trim the edges neatly, then re-roll the trimmings, cut out leaves and use to decorate the edges.

5 Spread the filling in the pastry case and bake for 25–30 minutes, or until the pastry is crisp.

APPLE MERINGUE TART

Like pears, quinces substitute well in most apple recipes. If you ever find any quinces, this is the ideal tart to use them in.

INGREDIENTS

Serves 6
½ cup flour, sifted
¾ cup whole wheat flour, sifted
pinch of salt
½ cup superfine sugar
6 tbsp butter
1 egg, separated, plus 1 egg white
1½lb eating apples
juice of ½ lemon
2 tbsp butter
3 tbsp raw sugar

1 To make the pastry, sift the flours into a bowl with the salt, adding in the wheat flakes from the sieve. Add 1 tbsp of the superfine sugar and rub in the butter until the mixture resembles breadcrumbs.

2 Work in the egg yolk and, if necessary, 1–2 tbsp cold water. Knead lightly to bring together, wrap in plastic wrap and chill for 10–20 minutes.

3 Preheat the oven to 375°F. Roll out the pastry to a 9in round and use to line an 8in pie pan. Line with wax paper and fill with baking beans.

4 Bake for 15 minutes, then remove the paper and beans and cook for a further 5–10 minutes, until the pastry is crisp.

5 Meanwhile, peel, core and slice the apples; toss in lemon juice. Melt the butter, add the raw sugar and fry the apple until golden and just tender. Arrange in the pastry case.

6 Preheat the oven to 425°F. Whisk the egg whites until stiff. Whisk in half the remaining superfine sugar, then fold in the rest. Pipe over the apples. Bake for 6–7 minutes. Serve hot or cold with cream or ice cream.

APRICOT AND PEAR FILO ROULADE

This is a very quick way of making a strudel – normally, very time consuming to do – it tastes delicious all the same!

INGREDIENTS

Serves 4–6

⅔ cup ready-to-eat dried apricots, chopped
2 tbsp apricot preserve
1 tsp lemon juice
¼ cup brown sugar
2 medium-sized pears, peeled, cored and chopped
½ cup ground almonds
2 tbsp slivered almonds
8 sheets filo pastry
2 tbsp butter, melted
confectioner's sugar, to dust

1 Put the apricots, apricot preserve, lemon juice, brown sugar and pears into a pan and heat gently, stirring, for 5–7 minutes.

2 Remove from the heat and cool. Mix in the ground and slivered almonds. Preheat the oven to 400°F. Melt the butter in a pan.

3 Lightly grease a cookie sheet. Layer the pastry on the cookie sheet, brushing each layer with butter.

4 Spoon the filling down the pastry just to one side of the center and within 1in of each end. Lift the other side of the pastry up by sliding a spatula underneath.

5 Fold this pastry over the filling, tucking the edge under. Seal the ends neatly and brush all over with butter again.

6 Bake for 15–20 minutes, until golden. Dust with confectioner's sugar and serve hot with cream.

POPPYSEED CUSTARD WITH RED FRUIT

INGREDIENTS

Serves 6
2½ cups milk
2 eggs
1–2 tbsp sugar
1 tbsp poppyseeds
4oz each of strawberries,
   raspberries and blackberries
1–2 tbsp light brown sugar
4 tbsp grape juice

1 Preheat the oven to 300°F. Heat the milk until scalding, but do not boil. Beat the eggs in a bowl with the sugar and poppyseeds until creamy.

2 Whisk the milk into the egg mixture until very well blended. Place a buttered soufflé dish in a shallow roasting pan, half-filled with hot water.

3 Pour the custard into the soufflé dish and bake for 50–60 minutes, until just set and the top is golden.

4 While the custard is baking, mix the fruit with the brown sugar and fruit juice. Chill until ready to serve with the warm baked custard.

CARAMEL RICE PUDDING

If you thought rice pudding had gone out of fashion, you are mistaken: it has certainly come back in again, especially when served with crunchy fresh fruit.

INGREDIENTS

Serves 4
¼ cup short grain pudding rice
5 tbsp raw sugar
pinch of salt
14oz can condensed milk made up to
   2½ cups with water
1 tbsp butter
1 small fresh pineapple
2 crisp eating apples
2 tsp lemon juice

1 Preheat the oven to 300°F. Put the rice in a strainer and wash thoroughly under cold water. Drain well and put into a lightly greased soufflé dish.

2 Add 2 tbsp of the raw sugar and the salt to the dish. Pour on the diluted condensed milk and stir gently.

3 Dot the surface of the rice with butter and bake for 2 hours, then leave to cool for 30 minutes.

4 Meanwhile, peel, core and slice the apples and pineapple, then cut the pineapple into chunks. Toss the fruit in lemon juice and set aside.

5 Preheat the broiler and sprinkle the remaining sugar over the rice. Broil for 5 minutes until the sugar has caramelized. Leave the rice to stand for 5 minutes to allow the caramel to harden, then serve with the fresh fruit.

Bitter Marmalade Pudding

Ingredients

Serves 4–6

¾ cup sugar
¾ cup soft margarine
3 eggs, beaten
1½ cups self-rising flour, sifted
¼–½ tsp ground ginger
grated rind and juice of 1 large orange
5 tbsp thick-cut marmalade

1 Cream together the sugar and margarine until light and fluffy.

2 Gradually beat in the eggs, beating well between each addition. Fold in the flour and ginger, then the orange rind and juice. Stir 2 tbsp of the marmalade into the mixture.

3 Tip the remaining 3 tbsp marmalade into the base of a heatproof bowl. Carefully spoon the pudding mixture on top and smooth the surface.

4 Cover the bowl with wax paper and foil which has been pleated to allow the mixture to rise. Secure the paper with string and steam the pudding for 2 hours, topping up the water in the base of the steamer when necessary.

5 Unmould the pudding on to a warmed serving plate and serve hot with custard or cream.

Apple and Golden Raisin Pie

You can't beat a traditional apple pie, with a pastry topping which is sweet and juicy underneath, yet crisp and flaky on top.

Ingredients

Serves 4–6

2lb cooking apples, peeled, cored and sliced
2 tsp ground cinnamon
⅔ cup golden raisins
5 tbsp sugar
12oz ready-made puff or flaky pastry
1 egg, beaten

1 Preheat the oven to 425°F. Mix the apples, cinnamon and raisins together, add the sugar (reserving 1–2 tsp for sprinkling) and pile into a 5 cup pie dish.

2 Roll out the pastry to 1in wider than the pie dish and cut a ½in strip off all round the edge. Dampen the rim of the dish and press the pastry strip around the rim.

3 Brush this strip with egg and lift the pastry carefully on top. Seal and trim the edges, fluting them neatly or press up with a knife. Brush the top with beaten egg and use any extra pastry to decorate. Brush with egg again and bake for 20 minutes.

4 Reduce the oven temperature to 375°F. Brush the top with egg again and cook for a further 15–20 minutes, until the top is flaky and golden. Sprinkle with the reserved sugar and serve hot.

COLD DESSERTS

Many cold desserts can easily be turned into special-occasion dishes just by the way you present them. And many dishes, which at first glance, may seem quite elaborate, are often quick and easy enough for any family meal – if you present them more simply. For instance, Crème Brulée, made the cheat's way, can be prepared very quickly, and Blackberry and Apple Romanoff can be mixed together in minutes, then once frozen, it can be served very simply from the bowl in scoops, or turned out and decorated if you prefer. Other desserts, such as Lemon Soufflé with Blackberries, and Pineapple and Strawberry Pavlova are perfect for dinner parties – they are simple to make, and can be prepared well ahead, ready to add the finishing touches just before serving.

FROZEN STRAWBERRY MOUSSE CAKE

Children love this cake –
because it is pink and pretty, and
it is just like an ice cream treat.

INGREDIENTS

Serves 4–6

15oz can strawberries in syrup
1 package powdered gelatine
6 trifle sponge cakes
3 tbsp strawberry preserve
⅞ cup crème fraîche or sour cream
⅞ cup whipped cream, to decorate

1 Strain the syrup from the strawberries into a large heatproof bowl. Sprinkle over the gelatine and stir well. Stand the bowl in a pan of hot water and stir until the gelatine has dissolved.

2 Leave to cool, then chill for just under 1 hour, until beginning to set. Meanwhile, cut the sponge cakes in half lengthwise and spread the cut surfaces with the strawberry preserve.

3 Slowly whisk the crème fraîche or cream into the strawberry jelly, then whisk in the canned strawberries. Line a deep, 8in loose-based cake pan with wax paper.

4 Pour half the strawberry mousse mixture into the pan, arrange the sponge cakes over the surface, and then spoon over the remaining mousse mixture, pushing down any sponge cakes which rise up.

5 Freeze for 1–2 hours until firm. Unmold the cake and carefully remove the lining paper. Transfer to a serving plate. Decorate with whirls of cream and a few strawberry leaves and a fresh strawberry, if you have them.

LEMON SOUFFLÉ WITH BLACKBERRIES

The simple fresh taste of the cold lemon mousse combines well with the rich blackberry sauce, and the color contrast looks wonderful, too. Blueberries or raspberries make equally delicious alternatives to blackberries.

INGREDIENTS

Serves 6
grated rind of 1 lemon and juice of 2 lemons
1 package powdered gelatine
5 eggs, separated
10 tbsp sugar
few drops vanilla extract
1⅔ cups whipping cream

For the sauce
6oz blackberries (fresh or frozen)
2–3 tbsp sugar
few fresh blackberries and blackberry leaves, to decorate

1 Place the lemon juice in a small pan and heat through. Sprinkle on the gelatine and leave to dissolve or heat further until clear. Allow to cool.

2 Put the lemon rind, egg yolks, sugar and vanilla into a large bowl and whisk until the mixture is very thick, pale and creamy.

3 Whisk the egg whites until stiff and almost peaked. Whip the cream until stiff and holding its shape.

4 Stir the gelatine mixture into the yolks, then fold in the whipped cream and lastly the egg whites. When lightly but thoroughly blended, turn into a 6 cup soufflé dish and freeze for 2 hours.

5 To make the sauce, place the blackberries in a pan with the sugar and cook for 4–6 minutes until the juices begin to run and all the sugar has dissolved. Pass through a sieve to remove the seeds, then chill until ready to serve.

6 When the soufflé is almost frozen, but still spoonable, scoop or spoon out on to individual plates and serve with the blackberry sauce.

RASPBERRY AND CRANBERRY JELLY

INGREDIENTS

Serves 6–8

3oz package raspberry Jello or 4oz
  raspberry jelly
1 cup raspberry and cranberry juice
4oz fresh strawberries
4oz raspberries (fresh or frozen)
1 large red-skinned apple, cored and
  chopped

1 Tip the Jello or jelly into a heatproof measuring jug and pour on ⅔ cup boiling water. Stir until dissolved. Then pour in the raspberry and cranberry juice and leave until beginning to set.

2 Hull and halve or quarter the strawberries, depending on their size. If using frozen raspberries, leave them in the freezer until you put the jelly to set. Prepare the apple at the last moment.

3 Have ready a pretty 4 cup mold, rinsed out with cold water. When the jelly is beginning to thicken, stir in the fruits. (With frozen raspberries it will set almost immediately, so work quickly.) Spoon into the mold and chill until set.

4 Turn out the jelly on to a plate and serve with custard, ricotta or frozen yogurt.

BLACKBERRY AND APPLE ROMANOFF

Rich yet fruity, this dessert is popular with most people and very quick to make.

INGREDIENTS

Serves 6–8

12oz 3–4 sharp eating apples, peeled,
  cored and chopped
3 tbsp sugar
1 cup whipping cream
1 tsp grated lemon rind
6 tbsp Greek-style yogurt
2oz (4–6) crisp meringues,
  roughly crumbled
8oz blackberries (fresh or frozen)
whipped cream, a few blackberries and
  mint leaves, to decorate

1 Line a 4–5 cup ovenproof glass bowl with plastic wrap. Toss the apples into a pan with 2 tbsp sugar and cook for 2–3 minutes, or until softening. Mash with a fork and leave to cool.

2 Whip the cream and fold in the lemon rind, yogurt, the remaining sugar, apples and meringues.

3 Gently stir in the blackberries, then tip the mixture into the glass bowl and freeze for 1–3 hours.

4 Turn out on to a plate and remove the plastic wrap. Decorate with whirls of whipped cream, blackberries and mint leaves.

COOK'S TIP
This also makes a delicious ice cream, though the texture of the frozen berries makes it difficult to scoop if it is frozen for more than 4–6 hours.

APPLE AND MINT HAZELNUT SHORTCAKE

INGREDIENTS

Serves 8–10

1 cup whole wheat flour
4 tbsp ground hazelnuts
4 tbsp confectioner's sugar, sifted
10 tbsp sweet butter or margarine
3 sharp eating apples
1 tsp lemon juice
about 1–2 tbsp sugar, to taste
1 tbsp chopped fresh mint, or
    1 tsp dried
1 cup whipping cream or
    crème fraîche
few drops vanilla extract
few mint leaves and whole hazelnuts, to
    decorate

1 Process the flour, ground hazelnuts and confectioner's sugar with the butter in a food processor in short bursts, or rub the butter into the dry ingredients until they come together. (Don't overwork the mixture.) Bring the dough together, adding a very little iced water if necessary. Knead briefly, wrap in wax paper and chill for 30 minutes.

2 Preheat the oven to 325°F. Cut the dough in half and roll out each half, on a lightly floured surface, to a 7in round. Place on wax paper on baking sheets and bake for about 40 minutes, or until crisp. If browning too much, move them down in the oven to a lower shelf. Allow to cool.

3 Peel, core and chop the apples into a pan with the lemon juice. Add sugar to taste, then cook for 2–3 minutes, until just softening. Mash the apple gently with the chopped fresh mint and leave to cool.

4 Whip the cream with the vanilla extract. Place one shortcake round on a serving plate. Spread half the apple and half the cream or crème fraîche on top .

5 Place the second shortcake on top, then spread over the remaining apple and cream, swirling the top layer of cream gently. Decorate the top with mint leaves and a few whole hazelnuts, then serve at once.

LEMON CHEESECAKE ON BRANDY SNAPS

Cheating with ready-made brandy snaps gives a quick and crunchy golden base to a simple classic cheesecake mixture.

INGREDIENTS

Serves 8
3oz package lemon Jello
2 cups low fat cream cheese
2 tsp lemon rind
about ½ cup sugar
few drops vanilla extract
⅔ cup thick yogurt
8 brandy snaps
mint leaves and confectioner's sugar,
  to decorate

1 Dissolve the Jello in ½ cup boiling water in a heatproof measuring jug and, when clear, add sufficient cold water to make up to ⅔ cup. Chill until beginning to thicken. Line a 1lb loaf pan with plastic wrap.

2 Cream the low fat cream cheese with the lemon rind, sugar and vanilla extract and beat until light and smooth. Then fold in the thickening lemon jelly and the yogurt. Spoon into the prepared pan and chill until set. Preheat the oven to 325°F.

3 Place two or three brandy snaps at a time on a baking sheet. Place in the oven for no more than 1 minute, until soft enough to unroll and flatten out completely. Leave on a cold plate or tray to harden again. Repeat with the remaining brandy snaps.

4 To serve, turn the cheesecake out on to a board with the help of the plastic wrap. Cut into eight slices and place one slice on each brandy snap base. Decorate with mint leaves and sprinkle with confectioner's sugar.

COOK'S TIP
If you don't have any brandy snaps on hand, you could serve this cheesecake on thin slices of moist ginger cake, or on other thin, crisp cookies.

CHOCOLATE FLAKE ICE CREAM

It doesn't matter whether or not you have an ice cream machine for this recipe – it's so quick, and just needs occasional whisking. Either bitter chocolate cookies or a hot apricot sauce would be a delicious accompaniment.

INGREDIENTS

Serves 6
1¼ cups whipping cream, chilled
6 tbsp thick yogurt
5–6 tbsp sugar
few drops vanilla extract
10 tbsp flaked or coarsely grated
  chocolate

1 Have ready a 3–4 cup freezer container, preferably with a lid. Prepare a place in the freezer so you can easily reach it.

2 Softly whip the cream in a large bowl and fold in the yogurt, sugar, vanilla extract and chocolate. Stir gently to mix thoroughly and then transfer to the freezer container.

3 Smooth the top of the ice cream, then cover and freeze. Gently stir with a fork every half hour or so until it is too hard to stir – this may take up to 4 hours. Serve in scoops.

MANGO AND RASPBERRY FOOL

INGREDIENTS

Serves 4–6
1 ripe mango
1 tbsp lemon juice
8oz raspberries, fresh, or frozen and
  defrosted
sugar, to taste
2 egg whites
⅔ cup whipping cream

2 Set aside a few raspberries for decoration. Add the remainder to the mango and purée in a food processor until smooth. Sieve thoroughly into a large bowl and sweeten to taste.

3 Whisk the egg whites stiffly and whip the cream into soft peaks. Fold them both gently into the fruit purée. When well blended, spoon into glasses and chill. Serve decorated with the reserved raspberries.

1 Peel the mango and then cut the flesh away from the central pit and place in a bowl. Sprinkle on the lemon juice.

COOK'S TIP
When fresh mangoes are not available, use two large ripe peaches or nectarines, or about 8oz fresh, ripe apricots.

PINEAPPLE AND STRAWBERRY PAVLOVA

This is a gooey pavlova which doesn't usually hold a perfect shape, but it has a wonderful marshmallow texture.

―――― INGREDIENTS ――――

Serves 6
5 egg whites, at room temperature
pinch of salt
1 tsp cornstarch
1 tbsp vinegar
few drops of vanilla extract
1½ cups sugar
1 cup whipping cream, whipped
6oz fresh pineapple, cut into chunks
6oz fresh strawberries, halved
strawberry leaves, to decorate

1 Preheat the oven to 325°F. Line a baking sheet with wax paper.

2 Put the egg whites in a large bowl and whisk until holding stiff peaks. Add the salt, cornstarch, vinegar and vanilla extract; whisk again until stiff.

3 Gently whisk in half the sugar, then carefully fold in the rest. Spoon the meringue on to the baking sheet and swirl into an 8in round with the back of a large spoon.

4 Bake for 20 minutes, then reduce the oven temperature to 300°F and bake for a further 40 minutes until the meringue is dry.

5 Transfer to a serving plate while still warm, then leave to cool. When ready to serve, fill with whipped cream, chunks of pineapple and halved strawberries and decorate with strawberry leaves, if you have them.

> COOK'S TIP
> You can also cook this in a deep, 8in loose-based cake pan. Cover the base with wax paper and grease the sides.

TANGERINE TRIFLE

An unusual variation on a traditional trifle – of course, you can add a little alcohol if you wish.

────── INGREDIENTS ──────

Serves 4

5 trifle sponges, halved lengthwise
2 tbsp apricot preserve
15–20 Amaretti biscuits
3oz package tangerine Jello or 4oz
*   tangerine jelly*
11oz can mandarin oranges, drained,
*   reserving juice*
2½ cups ready-made custard
whipped cream and shreds of orange
*   rind, to decorate*
sugar, for sprinkling

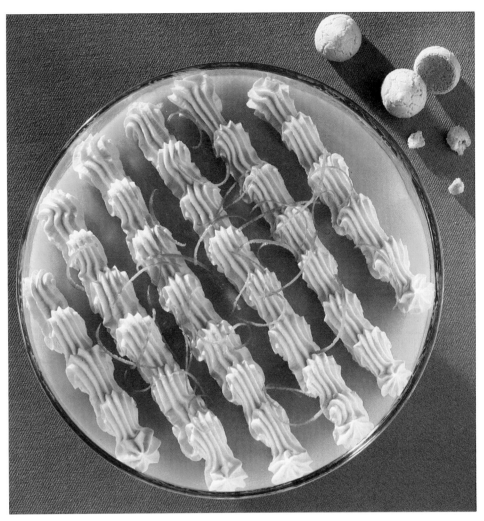

1 Spread the halved sponge cakes with apricot preserve and arrange in the base of a deep serving bowl or glass dish. Sprinkle over the Amarettis.

2 Tip the Jello or jelly into a heat-proof jug, add the juice from the canned mandarins and dissolve in a pan of hot water or in the microwave. Stir until the liquid clears.

3 Make up to 2 cups with ice cold water, stir well and leave to cool, for up to 30 minutes. Scatter the mandarin oranges over the cake and Amarettis

4 Pour the jelly over the mandarin oranges, cake and ratafias and chill for 1 hour, or more.

5 When the jelly has set, pour the custard over the top and chill again.

6 When ready to serve, pipe the whipped cream over the custard. Wash the orange rind shreds, sprinkle them with sugar and use to decorate the trifle.

ALMOST INSTANT BANANA PUDDING

INGREDIENTS

Serves 6–8

4 thick slices ginger cake
6 bananas, sliced
2 tbsp lemon juice
1¼ cups whipping cream or ricotta
4 tbsp fruit juice
3–4 tbsp soft brown sugar

1 Break the cake up into chunks and arrange in an ovenproof dish. Slice the bananas and toss in the lemon juice.

2 Whip the cream and, when firm, gently whip in the juice. (If using ricotta, just gently stir in the juice.) Fold in the bananas and spoon the mixture over the ginger cake.

3 Top with the sugar and place under a hot broiler for 2–3 minutes to caramelize. Chill to set firm again if you wish, or serve when required.

GINGER AND ORANGE CRÈME BRÛLÉE

This is a useful way of cheating at crème brûlée! Most people would never know unless you overchill the custard, or keep it more than a day, but there's little risk of that!

INGREDIENTS

Serves 4–5

2 eggs and 2 egg yolks
1¼ cups light cream
2 tbsp sugar
1 tsp powdered gelatine
finely grated rind and juice of ½ orange
1 large piece preserved ginger, finely chopped
3–4 tbsp confectioner's or superfine sugar

1 Whisk the eggs and yolks together until pale. Bring the cream and sugar to the boil, remove from the heat and sprinkle on the gelatine. Stir until the gelatine has dissolved and then pour the cream mixture onto the eggs, whisking all the time.

2 Add the orange rind, a little juice to taste, and the chopped ginger.

3 Pour into 4 or 5 ramekin dishes, or one larger flameproof serving dish and chill until set.

4 Some time before serving, sprinkle the sugar generously over the top of the custard and put under a very hot broiler. Watch closely for the couple of moments it takes for the tops to caramelize. Allow to cool before serving.

COOK'S TIP
For a milder ginger flavor, just add up to 1 tsp ground ginger instead of the preserved ginger.

Chilled Chocolate Pie

This is a very rich family dessert, but it is also designed to use up the occasional leftover! You don't need to eat it in a rush – it keeps very well.

Ingredients

Serves 6–8

½ cup butter, melted
8oz ginger cookies, finely crushed
1 cup stale sponge cake crumbs
4–5 tbsp orange juice
½ cup pitted dates, warmed
¼ cup finely chopped nuts
6oz bitter chocolate
1¼ cups whipping cream
grated chocolate and confectioner's
    sugar, to serve

1 Mix together the butter and ginger cookie crumbs, then pack around the sides and base of a 7in loose-based pie pan. Chill while making the filling.

2 Put the cake crumbs into a large bowl with the orange juice and leave to soak. Mash the warm dates thoroughly and blend into the cake crumbs along with the nuts.

3 Melt the chocolate with 3–4 tbsp of the cream. Softly whip the rest of the cream, then fold in the melted chocolate.

4 Stir the cream and chocolate mixture into the crumbs and mix well. Pour into the cookie crust case, mark into portions and leave to set. Scatter over the grated chocolate and dust with confectioner's sugar. Serve cut in wedges.

Autumn Fruit Salad

Despite the name, you can make a version of this fruit salad all year round – just change the fruit to suit the season.

Ingredients

Serves 4

2 tbsp sugar, plus extra to taste
juice of 1 lemon
1 red-skinned apple, cored and sliced
1 green-skinned apple, cored and
    sliced
1 pear, peeled, cored and sliced
⅔ cup apple or pear juice
4 plums, pitted and halved or
    quartered
4oz fresh raspberries, blackberries or
    blueberries

1 Dissolve the sugar in the lemon juice in a large bowl. As you prepare the apples and pear, put them straight into the lemon syrup.

2 Pour over the apple juice, cover the bowl closely and leave in a dark place for 2–6 hours.

3 A little while before serving, stir in the rest of the fruit and a little more sugar to taste.

CAKES AND COOKIES

Home baking never goes out of style, because it just happens to be the cheapest and most enjoyable way of giving our families and ourselves the cakes and biscuits that we really like. Here, there are not only old favorites to cook, such as Chocolate-Orange Cake, Date and Nut Loaf, Ginger Cookies, and Sticky Date and Apple Bars, but also some exciting new ideas to try, such as the sweet and tangy Pineapple and Apricot Cake, Coconut Meringues, and the very tasty Blueberry Streusel. In fact, there are cakes and cookies to suit everyone, and for all sorts of occasions – from breakfast through to late night munchies.

PINEAPPLE AND APRICOT CAKE

Serves 10–12
¾ cup sweet butter
¾ cup sugar
3 eggs, beaten
few drops vanilla extract
2 cups cake flour, sifted
¼ tsp salt
1½ tsp baking powder
1⅓ cups ready-to-eat dried apricots,
  chopped
½ cup each chopped crystalized ginger
  and crystalized pineapple
grated rind and juice of ½ orange
grated rind and juice of ½ lemon
a little milk

1 Preheat the oven to 350°F. Double line an 8in round or 7in square cake pan. Cream the butter and sugar together until light and fluffy.

2 Gradually beat the eggs into the creamed mixture with the vanilla extract, beating well after each addition. Sift together the flour, salt and baking powder, and add a little with the last of the egg, then fold in the rest.

3 Fold in the fruit, ginger and fruit rinds gently, then add sufficient fruit juice and milk to give a fairly soft dropping consistency.

4 Spoon into the prepared pan and smooth the top with a wet spoon. Bake for 20 minutes, then reduce the heat to 325°F for a further 1½–2 hours, or until firm to the touch and a skewer comes out of the center clean. Leave the cake to cool in the tin, turn out and wrap in fresh paper before storing in an airtight tin.

COOK'S TIP
This is not a long-keeping cake, but it does freeze, well-wrapped in wax paper and then foil.

ONE-MIX CHOCOLATE SPONGE CAKE

For family suppers and ever-open mouths, quick and easy favorites, like this chocolate cake, are invaluable.

INGREDIENTS

Serves 8–10
¾ cup soft margarine, at room temperature
½ cup sugar
4 tbsp corn syrup
1½ cups self-rising flour, sifted
3 tbsp cocoa powder, sifted
½ tsp salt
3 eggs, beaten
little milk (optional)
⅔ cup whipping cream
1–2 tbsp fine shred marmalade
sifted confectioner's sugar, to decorate

1 Preheat the oven to 350°F. Lightly grease or line two 7in cake pans. Place the margarine, sugar, syrup, flour, cocoa powder, salt and eggs in a large bowl or food processor and cream together until well blended. (In a processor use the slowest speed or frequent short bursts.)

COOK'S TIP
If you are filling up the freezer, this cake is ideal. Wrap the sponges in plastic wrap and store for up to six months. Defrost for 2 hours before sandwiching the cake with the filling.

2 If the mixture seems a little thick, stir in 1–2 tbsp milk, until you have a soft dropping consistency. Spoon the mixture into the prepared pans and bake for about 30 minutes, changing shelves if necessary after 15 minutes, until the tops are just firm and the cakes are springy to the touch.

3 Leave the cakes to cool for 5 minutes, then remove from the pans and leave to cool completely on a wire rack.

4 Whip the cream and fold in the marmalade, then use to sandwich the two cakes together and sprinkle the top with sifted confectioner's sugar.

HONEY APPLE CAKE

This is a moist cutting cake – perfect for everyday eating. You could also make it with pears in place of the apple for a change.

INGREDIENTS

Serves 8
½ cup butter or margarine
¾ cup honey
3 eggs, beaten
1½ cups flour
1½ cups whole wheat flour
½ tsp salt
½ tsp soda
few drops vanilla extract
1 large apple, peeled, cored and finely diced
3–4 tbsp milk or apple juice
few apple slices and 2–3 tbsp raw sugar, for topping

1 Preheat the oven to 350°F. Lightly grease a 7in square or 8in round cake pan. Cream the butter and honey together until soft and pale. Beat in the eggs a little at a time, then fold in the dry ingredients with the vanilla extract.

2 When well mixed, stir in the apple and enough of the milk or apple juice to give a soft dropping consistency. Spoon the mixture into the tin and smooth over the top.

3 Bake for 30 minutes, then arrange the apple slices on the top and sprinkle generously with raw sugar. Continue cooking for a further 30 minutes, or until the cake is just firm when you press it.

4 Turn off the heat and leave to cool in the oven. Remove from the pan before it is completely cold and wrap in foil to store. Serve sliced, with butter or simply on its own.

OAT AND APRICOT CLUSTERS

Here is a variation on an old favorite which children can easily make themselves, so have plenty of the dried fruits and nuts ready for them to add in.

INGREDIENTS

Makes 12
4 tbsp butter or margarine
4 tbsp honey
4 tbsp medium oatmeal
4 tbsp chopped ready-to-eat dried apricots
1 tbsp banana chips
1 tbsp dried shreds of coconut
2–3 cups cornflakes or Rice Krispies

1 Place the butter or margarine and honey in a small pan and warm over a low heat, stirring until well blended.

2 Add the oatmeal, apricots, banana chips, coconut and cornflakes or Rice Krispies and mix well.

3 Spoon the mixture into twelve paper cupcake cups, piling it up roughly. Transfer to a baking sheet, or tray and chill until set and firm.

COOK'S TIP
You can change the ingredients, according to what's in your store-cupboard – try peanuts, pecan nuts, raisins or dates.

COCONUT MERINGUES

Make these meringues tiny to serve with a fruit salad, or make the bigger ones and sandwich with cream or crème fraîche to serve for tea.

INGREDIENTS

Makes 16 larger meringues
3 egg whites, at room temperature
1½ cups sugar
½ cup unsweetened shredded
  coconut
whipped cream or crème fraîche, and
  lemon curd (optional), to serve

1 Preheat the oven to 325°F. Whisk the egg whites in a large, clean bowl, until stiff. Whisk in half the sugar until smooth and glossy.

2 Carefully fold in the rest of the sugar and the coconut with a metal spoon. When well blended, place tablespoonfuls well apart on wax paper on baking sheets.

3 Bake the meringues for 20 minutes, then change the baking sheets over and reduce the temperature to 275°F for a further 40 minutes, or until crisp and slightly golden.

4 Remove the meringues from the paper while they are still warm. Transfer to a wire rack and leave to cool before sandwiching with whipped cream, crème fraîche, or a mixture of whipped cream and lemon curd.

> **COOK'S TIP**
> You could use this mixture to make one large meringue gâteau. Spread out the mixture in two 7in rounds and bake as above, then sandwich with one of the suggested fillings.

CHOCOLATE-ORANGE CAKE

INGREDIENTS

Makes 1 cake
½ cup soft margarine
4 tbsp sugar
2 eggs, beaten
few drops vanilla extract
1 tbsp ground almonds
1 cup self-rising flour, sifted
1 tbsp cocoa powder, sifted
2–3 tbsp milk
grated rind and juice of ½ orange
1 jar chocolate and nut spread
8oz white almond paste

1 Preheat the oven to 350°F. Grease and line a 7in square cake tin. Arrange a double piece of foil across the middle of the tin, to divide it into two equal oblongs.

2 Cream the margarine and sugar together. Then beat in the eggs, vanilla extract and ground almonds.

3 Divide the mixture evenly into two halves. Fold half of the flour into one half, along with the orange rind and sufficient juice to give a soft dropping consistency.

4 Fold the rest of the flour and the cocoa powder into the other half of the mixture along with sufficient milk to give a soft dropping consistency. Fill the tin with the two mixes and flatten the top with a wetted spoon.

5 Bake for 15 minutes, then reduce the heat to 325°F, for a further 20–30 minutes, or until the top is just firm. Leave to cool in the tin for a few minutes.

6 Turn out on to a board, cut each cake into two strips. Trim so they are even, then leave to cool.

7 Using the chocolate and nut spread, sandwich the cakes together, chocolate and orange side by side, then orange and chocolate on top. Spread the sides with more of the chocolate and nut spread.

8 Roll out the white almond paste on a board lightly dusted with cornstarch to a rectangle 7in wide and long enough to wrap all round the cake. Wrap the almond paste carefully around the cake, putting the join underneath. Press to seal.

9 Mark a criss-cross pattern on the almond paste with a knife, then pinch up the corners if you wish. Store in a cool place. Serve, cut across into thick slices.

RASPBERRY MUFFINS

Makes 10–12
1 cup self-rising flour
1 cup whole wheat self-rising flour
3 tbsp sugar
½ tsp salt
2 eggs, beaten
scant 1 cup milk
4 tbsp melted butter
6oz raspberries, fresh or frozen
(defrosted for less than 30 minutes)

1 Preheat the oven to 375°F. Lightly grease the muffin pan, or use paper cupcake cups. Sift the dry ingredients together, then tip back in the whole wheat flakes from the sieve.

2 Beat the eggs, milk and melted butter together and stir into the dry ingredients to make a thick batter.

3 Stir in the raspberries gently and spoon into the pans or paper cups. (If you are using frozen raspberries, work quickly as the cold berries make the mixture solidify.) If you mix too much the raspberries begin to disintegrate and color the dough.

4 Bake for 30 minutes, until well risen and just firm. Serve warm or cool.

FAIRY CAKES WITH BLUEBERRIES

This luxurious way to treat fairy cakes means you can also serve them to adults and guests. It is also a little healthier than buttercream!

Makes 12–14 cakes
½ cup soft margarine
8 tbsp sugar
1 tsp grated lemon rind
pinch of salt
2 eggs, beaten
1 cup self-rising flour, sifted
½ cup whipping cream, whipped
3–4oz blueberries, fresh or frozen
sifted confectioner's sugar, for dusting

1 Preheat the oven to 375°F. Cream the margarine, sugar, lemon rind and salt in a large bowl until pale and fluffy.

2 Gradually beat in the eggs, then fold in the flour until well mixed. Spoon the mixture into 8–10 cupcake cups on baking sheets and bake for 15–20 minutes, until just golden.

3 Leave the cakes to cool, then scoop out a circle of sponge from the top of each using the point of a small, sharp knife and set them aside.

4 Place a spoonful of cream in each sponge, plus 2–3 blueberries. Replace the lids at an angle and dust with sifted confectioner's sugar.

DATE AND NUT LOAF

INGREDIENTS

Makes 2 x 1lb loaves

2 cups flour
2 cups whole wheat flour
1 tsp salt
6 tbsp brown sugar
1 package Rapid-Rise yeast
4 tbsp butter or margarine
1 tbsp black molasses
4 tbsp malt extract
1 cup lukewarm milk
½ cup chopped dates
½ cup chopped nuts
½ cup golden raisins
½ cup raisins
2 tbsp honey, to glaze

1 Sift the flours and salt into a large bowl, then tip in the wheat flakes that are caught in the sieve. Stir in the sugar and yeast.

2 Put the butter or margarine in a small pan with the molasses and malt extract. Stir over a low heat until melted. Leave to cool, then combine with the milk.

3 Stir the liquid into the dry ingredients and knead thoroughly for 15 minutes until the dough is elastic. (If you have a dough blade on your food processor, follow the manufacturers' instructions for timings.)

4 Knead in the fruits and nuts. Transfer the dough to an oiled bowl, cover with plastic wrap and leave in a warm place for about 1½ hours, until the dough has doubled in size.

5 Grease two 1lb loaf pans. Knock back the dough and knead lightly. Divide in half, form into loaves and place in the pans. Cover and leave in a warm place for about 30 minutes, until risen. Meanwhile, preheat the oven to 375°F.

6 Bake for 35–40 minutes, until well risen and sounding hollow when tapped underneath. Cool on a wire rack. Brush with honey while warm.

ORANGE WHEAT LOAF

Perfect just with butter as a breakfast or tea bread and lovely for banana sandwiches.

— INGREDIENTS —

Makes one 1lb loaf
2¼ cups whole wheat flour
½ tsp salt
2 tbsp butter
2 tbsp light brown sugar
½ package Rapid-Rise yeast
grated rind and juice of ½ orange

1 Sift the flour into a large bowl and return any wheat flakes from the sieve. Add the salt and rub in the butter lightly with your fingertips.

2 Stir in the sugar, yeast and orange rind. Pour the orange juice into a measuring jug and make up to ⅞ cup with hot water (the liquid should not be more than hand hot).

3 Stir the liquid into the flour and mix to a soft ball of dough. Knead gently on a lightly floured surface until quite smooth.

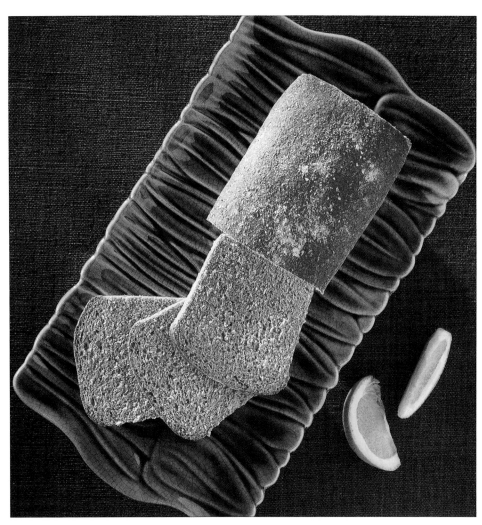

4 Place the dough in a greased 1lb loaf pan and leave in a warm place until nearly doubled in size. Preheat the oven to 425°F.

5 Bake the bread for 30–35 minutes, or until it sounds hollow when you tap the loaf underneath. Tip out of the tin and cool on a wire rack.

> FREEZER NOTE
> To freeze, wrap tightly in foil when still warm, then leave to cool completely before freezing. Keeps for up to one year.

LEMONY PEANUT PAIRS

For those who don't like peanut butter, use a buttercream or chocolate and nut spread instead.

INGREDIENTS

Makes 8–10
3 tbsp light brown sugar
4 tbsp soft margarine
1 tsp grated lemon rind
¾ cup whole wheat flour
4 tbsp chopped crystalized
  pineapple
2 tbsp smooth peanut butter
sifted confectioner's sugar, for
  dusting

1 Preheat the oven to 375°F. Cream the sugar, margarine and lemon rind together in a small bowl until pale and fluffy.

2 Work in the flour and knead for 1–2 minutes until smooth. Roll out thinly on a lightly floured surface, cut into rounds and place on baking sheets.

3 Press on pieces of pineapple to decorate and bake for 15–20 minutes. Cool on the trays. Sandwich pairs together with a little peanut butter when cool, and dust with confectioner's sugar.

GINGER COOKIES

If your children enjoy cooking with you, mixing and rolling the dough, or cutting out different shapes, this is the ideal recipe to let them practice on.

INGREDIENTS

Makes about 16
8 tbsp brown sugar
½ cup soft margarine
pinch of salt
few drops vanilla extract
1⅓ cup whole wheat flour
1 tbsp cocoa powder, sifted
2 tsp ground ginger
a little milk
glacé icing and candied cherries, to
  decorate

1 Preheat the oven to 375°F. Cream the sugar, margarine, salt and vanilla extract together until very soft and light.

2 Work in the flour, cocoa powder and ginger, adding a little milk, if necessary, to bind the mixture. Knead lightly on a floured surface.

3 Roll out the dough on a lightly floured surface to about ¼in thick. Stamp out shapes using biscuit cutters and place on cookie sheets.

4 Bake the cookies for 10–15 minutes, leave to cool on the cookie sheets until firm, then transfer to a wire rack to cool completely. Decorate with the glacé icing and candied cherries.

BLUEBERRY STREUSEL

INGREDIENTS

Makes about 30 slices

8oz shortcrust pastry
½ cup flour
¼ tsp baking powder
3 tbsp butter or margarine
2 tbsp fresh white breadcrumbs
⅓ cup light brown sugar
¼ tsp salt
4 tbsp slivered or chopped almonds
4 tbsp blackberry or blueberry jelly
4oz blueberries, fresh or frozen

1 Preheat the oven to 350°F. Roll out the pastry on a lightly floured surface to line an 7 x 11in jelly roll pan. Prick the base with a fork evenly.

2 Rub together the flour, baking powder, butter or margarine, breadcrumbs, sugar and salt until really crumbly, then mix in the almonds.

3 Spread the pastry with the jelly, sprinkle with the blueberries, then cover evenly with the streusel topping, pressing down lightly. Bake for 30–40 minutes, reducing the temperature after 20 minutes to 325°F.

4 Remove from the oven when golden on the top and the pastry is cooked through. Cut into slices while still hot, then allow to cool.

STICKY DATE AND APPLE BARS

If possible allow this mixture to mature for 1–2 days before cutting – it will get stickier and better!

INGREDIENTS

Makes about 16 bars

½ cup margarine
4 tbsp dark brown sugar
4 tbsp corn syrup
4oz chopped dates
1¼ cups rolled oats
1 cup whole wheat self-rising flour
2 apples, peeled, cored and grated
1–2 tsp lemon juice
20–25 walnut halves

1 Preheat the oven to 375°F. Line a 7–8in square or rectangular loose-based cake pan. In a large pan heat the margarine, sugar, syrup and dates, stirring until the dates soften completely.

2 Gradually work in the oats, flour, apples and lemon juice until well mixed. Spoon into the pan and spread out evenly. Top with the walnut halves.

3 Bake for 30 minutes, then reduce the temperature to 325°F and bake for 10–20 minutes more, until firm to the touch and golden. Cut into squares or bars while still warm, or wrap in foil when nearly cold and keep for 1–2 days before eating.

INDEX